A Quiet Time
EXPERIENCE

PASSIONATE PRAYER

CATHERINE MARTIN

HARVEST HOUSE PUBLISHERS

EUGENE, OREGON

Cover by Koechel Peterson & Associates, Inc., Minneapolis, Minnesota

Cover photo © Xavi Arnau / iStockphoto

PASSIONATE PRAYER—A QUIET TIME EXPERIENCE
Copyright © 2009 by Catherine Martin
Published by Harvest House Publishers
Eugene, Oregon 97402
www.harvesthousepublishers.com

ISBN 978-0-7369-2379-8

Printed in the United States of America

09 10 11 12 13 14 15 16 17 / ML-SK / 10 9 8 7 6 5 4 3 2 1

To my dear friends and family
who have been so faithful to pray
for me over the years.

❧

I can't imagine where I would be
without your prayers to the Lord on my behalf.
Thank you for your love, your faithfulness to Christ,
and your passionate prayer.

I urge you, first of all, to pray.

1 TIMOTHY 2:1

❧ CONTENTS ❧

WEEK 8: Prayer When You Want to Go Higher

≈℧ INTRODUCTION ℧≈

A number of years ago, my friend Kelly and I drove to San Diego to research a retreat location for our women's ministries. The moment we got in the car we began talking about what was going on in our lives. We played worship music and occasionally just stopped our conversation to sing along. When we arrived at the resort, we received a guided tour of the facility, and then we had the rest of the day to ourselves. We walked along the harbor, talking about what God was doing in us. Finally, at the moment when we could go no further, we saw a bench beckoning us to sit awhile. For some time, we sat on that bench, watching the ships go in and out of the harbor, and talking about dreams for ministry that the Lord was laying on our hearts. I said, "Kelly, I am so filled with a burden for people to open the pages of the Bible and grow deep in their relationship with God."

Kelly prayed, *Lord, I ask that You will fulfill this dream of Catherine's, that You will open the doors of ministry for her.* Then Kelly shared her heart and her passion for prayer, that those in the church would become a praying people and that the church would become a house of prayer.

O Lord, I prayed, *thank You for how You are using Kelly in the body of Christ. Open the doors to use her in the lives of hundreds of thousands to encourage them in their life of prayer.* What a blessed, sacred time with my friend—sharing, laughing, worshipping the Lord. While driving back home, we sang worship songs with the CD volume up full blast, all the windows rolled down, enjoying the powerful presence of God.

Relationships are some of God's greatest blessings in life. Perhaps the most special part of any relationship is the time spent merely keeping company—sharing, talking, laughing, dreaming, questioning, complaining. Sometimes there is only silence. Sometimes we articulate deep thoughts and emotions; sometimes we chatter away about nothing in particular. I believe this "keeping company" in earthly relationships helps us understand the true nature of prayer. Prayer is much more than taking our requests to God. Prayer is our life with God—walking and talking with Him throughout each day of our lives.

You can see the biblical concept of "walking and talking" prayer in the life of Jesus. We know that Jesus "would often slip away to the wilderness and pray" (Luke 5:16). He made prayer a regular, definable priority, because in "the early morning, while it was still dark, Jesus got up, left the house, and went away to a secluded place, and was praying there" (Mark 1:35). Prayer was His practice; He prayed all the time. The writer of Hebrews sums up the prayer life of Jesus: "In the days of His flesh, He offered up both prayers and supplications with loud crying and tears to the

One able to save Him from death, and He was heard because of His piety" (Hebrews 5:7). Jesus, the Son of God, without sin, the heir of all things, the radiance of the glory of God, and the exact representation of God's nature, prayed. To me, His example defines prayer well and explains it in ways no other person can. He talked with His Father. And He walked with His Father. We see Him describing and demonstrating a life of constant prayer. He talked with God in such a profound way that His example motivated His disciples to ask, "Lord, teach us to pray" (Luke 11:1).

How can we learn to pray? I believe the psalms are a unique gift and blessing from God, giving us a window into the practice of prayer. Luther regarded Psalms as the prayer book of the Bible. Jesus clearly knew the psalms well, because in His most desperate hour, He used Psalms as His prayer book. And He included some of the psalmists' words as His own prayers. On the cross He cried, "My God, My God, why have You forsaken Me" (Matthew 27:46, quoting from Psalm 22:1) and "Father, into Your hands I commit My Spirit" (Luke 23:46, quoting from Psalm 31:5). We see that the disciples also quoted the psalms in their prayers (Acts 4:24-26, quoting from Psalm 2:1; 146:6). And Paul exhorted believers to "let the word of Christ richly dwell within you, with all wisdom teaching and admonishing one another with psalms and hymns and spiritual songs, singing with thankfulness in your hearts to God" (Colossians 3:16). Knowing and praying the psalms was clearly the constant practice of Jesus and the disciples. I believe no task in our devotional lives can so inspire us to pray, admonish us to pray, and teach us to pray than knowing and praying the psalms. They lift our prayers to greater heights and deepen the extent of our conversation with our Lord.

I discovered the power of prayer by knowing and praying the psalms one year while I was encountering a dark night of the soul. It was a time of profound loss—a home, a profession—and everything had changed. We had moved to a new city, where I knew no one. I felt so very alone, as if I had lost the smile and favor of God. I felt like the psalmist who said, "I am so troubled that I cannot speak" (Psalm 77:4). A silence came over me. I could not bring myself to speak with God. I wasn't angry; I was broken. I could barely open the pages of my Bible. What could I do in this time of dark, deep despair?

I opened to the psalms; I truly believe the Lord directed me to the psalms and no other place in the Bible. I began praying through Psalms, one by one, living in its corridors, walking the hallways laid out by David, the shepherd king; by Moses, who spoke with God face-to-face, as a friend; and by Asaph, one of David's worship leaders. Slowly, methodically, like a soothing balm to a wound, the Lord healed my heart and brought me to a higher place with Him. The psalmists became my prayer partners, showing me how to walk and talk with God.

Now I love the psalms—perhaps more than any other book in the Bible. Anyone who knows me knows of my love for the psalms. I quote them often to friends and acquaintances. I have written books based on the psalms. I have written messages on the psalms for my church and other churches. I am always on the lookout for a new commentary on the psalms to use in my quiet time—so much so that I love to read and pray from the psalms every day.

And so, back to the question, how can we learn to walk and talk with God? I believe the best way is to allow the psalmists to become our prayer partners, teaching us the art of walking and talking with God. The psalmists pray from the heart; they are passionate prayer warriors. In this book we are going to explore what I consider to be the finest, most eloquent prayers in the psalms, learning from the master prayer warriors themselves, the psalmists. These will be our prayer partners—David, Asaph, the sons of Korah, Moses, and unnamed others—all the blessed writers of the psalms.

Dietrich Bonhoeffer encourages us to allow the richness of God's Word to determine our prayers, not the poverty of our hearts. Of course, the Lord longs for us to pour out our hearts to Him in prayer. But the Word of God in the psalms will lead us on a new journey and inspire us to new prayers, deeper thoughts, and higher aspirations.

Every time God says something in the Bible, His words suggest a prayer. For example, when David prays for the people of Israel, "Fix their heart toward You" (1 Chronicles 29:18 NKJV), he gives us a new prayer: *O Lord, fix my heart toward You.* David cries out to the God who is everything to him, "I love You, O LORD, my strength. The LORD is my rock and my fortress, and my deliverer, My God, my rock, in whom I take refuge; My shield and the horn of my salvation, my stronghold" (Psalm 18:1). And I am given new words to express my own love for the Lord. I can use them almost exactly, verbatim, to describe my heart to my Lord. Or I can use them as a beginning and then elaborate with my own experience with God. *Lord, I love You. You are my deliverer. Thank You for giving me the psalms to heal my broken heart and bring me to a new place of joy and intimacy with You.*

I invite you to join me on a life-changing experience in the psalms, learning from the psalmists, allowing them to be your prayer partners and to teach you to walk and talk with God. This eight-week book is the companion to *Passionate Prayer*—a 30-day journey where we share together the great power of talking with God. In that book we learned how to walk and talk with God. Now we are going to experience prayer with the psalmists, our prayer partners. I am so excited to begin this adventure with you through some of my favorite psalms on prayer. We will adore God, confess sin, say thank You, pray for deliverance, and go to higher places with God.

This quiet time experience is designed for you. You have a busy life but recognize that quiet time with God is essential if you are to be your utmost for His highest. If you want to know the Lord intimately, spending time in His Word and in prayer is imperative. You will discover that all you need is your Bible and this book of quiet times for a rich time alone with the Lord. It is filled with devotional reading, devotional Bible study, hymns, journaling, prayer, and practical application. It is more than a simple devotional, more than a Bible study—it's quiet time! Each quiet time is organized according to the PRAYER Quiet Time Plan:

Prepare Your Heart

Read and Study God's Word

Adore God in Prayer

Yield Yourself to God

Enjoy His Presence

Rest in His Love

Each week consists of five days of quiet times and a devotional reading on days 6 and 7. Journal and prayer pages (adapted from the *Quiet Time Notebook*) are in the back of this book for your use during these quiet times. Companion messages are available on DVD from Quiet Time Ministries (www.quiettime.org). Use the discussion questions in the appendix of this book with a friend or a group.

As you engage in this quiet time experience, feel free to look at verses in other translations, look at the meaning of a particular word, or consult commentaries or study Bible notes. If you desire to learn more about how to have a quiet time, I encourage you to get my book *Six Secrets to a Powerful Quiet Time*. To learn more about different kinds of devotional Bible studies for your quiet time, I encourage you to read my *Knowing and Loving the Bible*.

As we begin these quiet times, I would like to ask you a basic question: Where are you? What has been happening in your life during the past year or so? What has been your life experience? What are you facing at present? What has God been teaching you? It is no accident that you are in this book of quiet times. Indeed, God has something He wants you to know, something that will change the whole landscape of your experience with Him. Watch for it, listen for it, and when you learn it, write it down and never let it go. Will you write a prayer in the form of a letter to the Lord in the space provided on the next page, expressing all that is on your heart and asking Him to speak to you in these quiet times?

My Letter to the Lord

PRAYING WITH THE PSALMISTS

1 TIMOTHY 2:1

The Psalter is the great school of prayer. Here we learn, first, what prayer means. It means praying according to the Word of God, on the basis of promises. Christian prayer takes its stand on the solid ground of the revealed Word.

DIETRICH BONHOEFFER

THE FIRST THING

I urge you, first of all, to pray.
1 TIMOTHY 2:1 NLT

PREPARE YOUR HEART

Many years ago, a woman, living in a small house in the poorest area of London, dared to pray. She didn't just pray one prayer, but talked with God constantly about her rebellious son. Her only source of income came from standing day after day over a washtub. So there she stood, working and praying, working and praying. She knew God would answer her prayers, and she never gave up the hope that her son would give his life to the Lord one day. She prayed until the day she died but never saw the answer, except from a distance, by faith. But God did indeed answer her prayers, and her son, a slave trader, became the sailor-preacher of London. John Newton brought thousands of people to Christ and has impacted literally millions with the hymn he wrote, "Amazing Grace," expressing his personal experience of the grace, mercy, and forgiveness of God.

Oh, how mighty were the prayers of that unknown woman, who was well-known to her God! And oh, how powerful are your prayers when you dare to draw near to God and talk with Him. Dear friend, as you embark on this quiet time experience, will you take a few moments and talk with God about your own life of prayer? Ask the Lord to teach you to pray.

READ AND STUDY GOD'S WORD

1. The priority of prayer is assumed throughout the Bible. One person who taught constantly about prayer was Paul the apostle. Read the following translations of Paul's words to his disciple Timothy in 1 Timothy 2:1-3, and underline words and phrases that are significant to you:

> "First of all, then, I urge that entreaties and prayers, petitions and thanksgivings, be made on behalf of all men, for kings and all who are in authority, so that we may lead a tranquil and quiet life in all godliness and dignity. This is good and acceptable in the sight of God our Savior."

> "First, I tell you to pray for all people, asking God for what they need and being

thankful to him. Pray for rulers and for all who have authority so that we can have quiet and peaceful lives full of worship and respect for God. This is good, and it pleases God our Savior" (NCV).

"I urge, then, first of all, that requests, prayers, intercession and thanksgiving be made for everyone—for kings and all those in authority, that we may live peaceful and quiet lives in all godliness and holiness. This is good, and pleases God our Savior" (NIV).

"I urge you, first of all, to pray for all people. Ask God to help them; intercede on their behalf, and give thanks for them. Pray this way for kings and all who are in authority so that we can live peaceful and quiet lives marked by godliness and dignity. This is good and pleases God our Savior" (NLT).

"First of all, then, I admonish and urge that petitions, prayers, intercessions, and thanksgivings be offered on behalf of all men, for kings and all who are in positions of authority or high responsibility, that [outwardly] we may pass a quiet and undisturbed life [and inwardly] a peaceable one in all godliness and reverence and seriousness in every way. For such [praying] is good and right, and [it is] pleasing and acceptable to God our Savior" (AMP).

"The first thing I want you to do is pray. Pray every way you know how, for everyone you know. Pray especially for rulers and their governments to rule well so we can be quietly about our business of living simply, in humble contemplation. This is the way our Savior God wants us to live" (MSG).

2. Look at the following verses and write out what you learn about the priority and practice of prayer.

Mark 1:35

Luke 5:15-16

Ephesians 6:18

Philippians 4:6-7

3. What is the most important truth you have learned about prayer today?

ADORE GOD IN PRAYER

Pray these words of David in Psalm 69:13, acknowledging the priority of prayer in your own life:

> "But as for me, my prayer is to You, O LORD, at an acceptable time;
> O God, in the greatness of Your lovingkindness,
> Answer me with Your saving truth."

YIELD YOURSELF TO GOD

The Word of the Father is a call to prayer. Everywhere in His Word God calls His children to the prayer life. "Ask, and ye shall receive." "And He spake a parable unto them that men ought always to pray and not to faint." "Pray, that ye enter not into temptation." "Enter into thy closet, shut the door and pray to thy Father." "After this manner therefore pray ye." "Pray ye the Lord of the Harvest." "Pray without ceasing." "Brethren, pray for us." "I will therefore that men pray." "Is any afflicted, let him pray"…If Christ, the only sinless man who ever walked the earth, lived a life of constant communion with the Father through prayer, how much must we weak, earth-bound mortals need it.[1]

JAMES H. McCONKEY

The great people of the earth today are the people who pray. I do not mean those who talk about prayer; nor those who say they believe in prayer; nor yet those who can explain about prayer; but I mean these people who *take* time and *pray*. They have not time. It must be taken from something else. This something else is important. Very important, and pressing, but still less important and less pressing than prayer. There are people that put prayer first, and group the other items in life's schedule around and after prayer. These are the people today who are doing the most for God; in winning souls; in solving problems; in awakening churches; in supplying both men and money for mission posts; in keeping fresh and strong these lives far off in sacrificial service on the foreign field where the thickest fighting is going on; in keeping the old earth sweet awhile longer.[2]

S.D. GORDON

Get into the habit of dealing with God about everything. Unless in the first waking moment of the day you learn to fling the door wide back and let God in, you will work on the wrong level all day; but swing the door wide open and pray to your Father in secret, and every public thing will be stamped with the presence of God.[3]

OSWALD CHAMBERS

ENJOY HIS PRESENCE

As you close your time with the Lord today, describe what you have learned about the priority of prayer. What would you like to see happen in your own life of prayer? Use the journal pages in the back of this book to record your thoughts.

REST IN HIS LOVE

"Early in the morning, long before daybreak, He got up and went out to a lonely spot, and stayed praying there" (Mark 1:35 WILLIAMS).

PASSIONATE ABOUT PRAYER

Hear, O LORD, and be gracious to me;
O LORD, be my helper.
You have turned for me my mourning into dancing;
You have loosed my sackcloth and girded me with gladness,
That my soul may sing praise to You and not be silent.
O LORD my God, I will give thanks to You forever.

PSALM 30:10-12

PREPARE YOUR HEART

Jim Elliot, missionary to the Auca Indians in Ecuador in the early 1950s, was a man of God seasoned in praying passionate prayers to God. When you read his journals, you immediately notice prayers written out in the experience of his everyday life. However, these prayers are no ordinary prayers, but deep, bold, and clearly laid out in a context well beyond the temporal, possessing the cadence of the heavenly and eternal. He prayed with such fervent desire to his Lord:

"God, I pray Thee, light these idle sticks of my life, and may I burn for Thee. Consume my life, my God, for it is Thine. I seek not a long life, but a full one, like You, Lord Jesus."

"Father, let me be weak that I might loose my clutch on everything temporal. My life, my reputation, my possessions, Lord, let me loose the tension of the grasping hand."

"O Christ, let me know Thee—let me catch glimpses of Thyself, seated and expectant in glory, let me rest there despite all wrong surging round me. Lead me in the right path, I pray."

"Father, take my life, yea, my blood if Thou wilt, and consume it with Thine enveloping fire. I would not save it, for it is not mine to save. Have it Lord, have it all. Pour out my life as an oblation for that world. Blood is only of value as it flows before Thine altar."

"God, deliver me from the dread asbestos of 'other things.' Saturate me with the oil of the Spirit that I may be a flame for You."

What does it take to become the kind of person who prays with such ardent, heartfelt passion to God? Much time spent alone with Him in His Word. Jim Elliot was experienced in the practice of the presence of God. Years before he ever set foot on the mission field, he opened his Bible, day by day, lived in it, and then walked and talked with God in prayer.

Every man or woman of God who has ever been seasoned at prayer has spent much time alone with God. David, the shepherd king and the man after God's own heart, knew how to walk and talk with God. Oh, that we might have a heart like David, who often drew near to God. Pray today that God will give you a heart to know Him, love Him, and keep company with Him.

READ AND STUDY GOD'S WORD

1. David's experience with the Lord extended all the way from childhood to teen years working in the fields as a shepherd. Who could have guessed that this young boy would eventually kill a giant in the name of the Lord (1 Samuel 17:31-54) and become king of Israel (2 Samuel 7)? In the writing of a prayer of praise and worship in Psalm 30, his main focus was the fact that he had prayed and God had answered. One practice prevalent in the life of David was prayer. Over and over again you see these words about David: "David inquired of the LORD" (see 1 Samuel 23:2-4; 30:8; 2 Samuel 2:1; 5:19,23). These words set the example of what we need to do regardless of what we face in life—pray.

Read Psalm 30 and write out everything you learn from David about prayer.

2. Did you notice that David described a time of trouble, when God seemed to be hiding His face (Psalm 30:7)? David's response was to cry out to God (Psalm 30:8,10). And what was the result? The Lord turned his mourning into dancing, and his soul was filled with gladness and thanksgiving (verses 11-12). Does God seem to be hiding His face from you? How does David's experience encourage you today?

3. Read the following short prayers of David and record what is most significant in each prayer

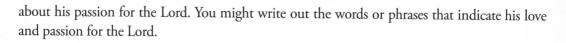

about his passion for the Lord. You might write out the words or phrases that indicate his love and passion for the Lord.

Psalm 3:3

Psalm 5:3

Psalm 8:1

Psalm 18:1

Psalm 19:14

4. How do you see David's heart for the Lord in his prayers?

ADORE GOD IN PRAYER

Pray these words of David in Psalm 5:3, expressing to the Lord your desire to make prayer your passion and priority:

"In the morning, O Lord, You will hear my voice;
In the morning I will order my prayer to You and eagerly watch."

YIELD YOURSELF TO GOD

Trouble is sent in mercy. It subserves a blessed end. It rouses a sleepy soul from a dangerous lethargy. It is a scourge which drives the careless to the mercy-seat. Here, when God's smile ceases, importunate petitions are in full activity. The gate of mercy opens to the returning knock. Faith is an inventive grace. From every trouble it can draw a plea. It here reasons, My destruction brings no glory to the courts of heaven: if my lips are silent in the grave, no longer can my praise be heard; my grateful tribute can no more set forth Thy truth. Then the prayer renews its strength, and cries for audience, mercy, help. Hence may our faith gather strong arguments to supplicate for joyful resurrection. Let our deep longings ever be to join the eternal hallelujahs, which are God's glory in the highest.[4]

HENRY LAW

ENJOY HIS PRESENCE

Whatever you are facing today, will you pray? Will you be encouraged by Henry Law and David, renew your strength, and cry out for God's audience, mercy, and help? Thank the Lord today for each truth He has taught you.

REST IN HIS LOVE

"I love you, O LORD, my strength" (Psalm 18:1).

PREOCCUPIED WITH PRAISE

You are resplendent, more majestic than the mountains of prey.
PSALM 76:4

PREPARE YOUR HEART

Praise is an outstanding characteristic in the psalms, forming a continuous thread through-out. Again and again, the psalmists praise the Lord. Praise expresses genuine appreciation for God's actions or character. Spurgeon says that praise "is the honey of life which a devout heart extracts from every bloom of providence and grace" and "the rehearsal of our eternal song." Have you learned this eternal song of praise? You will as you walk and talk with God through the words of the psalmists. Draw near to the Lord through the words of this Puritan prayer:

> Thou incomprehensible but prayer-hearing God,
> known, but beyond knowledge,
> revealed, but unrevealed,
> my wants and welfare draw me to thee,
> for thou hast never said, "Seek ye me in vain."
> To thee I come in my difficulties, necessities, distresses;
> possess me with thyself,
> with a spirit of grace and supplication,
> with a prayerful attitude of mind,
> with access into warmth of fellowship,
> so that in the ordinary concerns of life
> my thoughts and desires may rise to thee,
> and in habitual devotion I may find a resource that will
> soothe my sorrows, sanctify my successes,
> and qualify me in all ways for dealings with my fellow men.
> I bless thee that thou hast made me capable
> of knowing thee, the author of all being,
> of resembling thee, the perfection of all excellency,

of enjoying thee, the source of all happiness.
O God, attend me in every part of my arduous and trying pilgrimage;
I need the same counsel, defence, comfort I found at my beginning.
Let my religion be more obvious to my conscience,
more perceptible to those around.
While Jesus is representing me in heaven, may I reflect him on earth,
While he pleads my cause, may I show forth his praise.
Continue the gentleness of thy goodness toward me,
And whether I wake or sleep, let thy presence go with me,
thy blessing attend me.
Thou hast led me on and I have found thy promises true,
I have been sorrowful, but thou hast been my help,
fearful, but thou hast delivered me,
despairing, but thou hast lifted me up.
Thy vows are ever upon me,
And I praise thee, O God. [5]

READ AND STUDY GOD'S WORD

1. One of the great psalmists of the Bible is Asaph, appointed by David as the leader of the choirs that celebrated, thanked, and praised the Lord (1 Chronicles 16:4-5). Asaph wrote Psalms 50 and 73–83. He was a professional at praising the Lord and led many others during the reign of David to celebrate the Lord. Look at the following verses written by Asaph and write out what you learn from him about how to praise the Lord:

Psalm 73:25

Psalm 75:1

Psalm 76:4

Psalm 79:13

Psalm 81:1

2. The psalms are filled with praise to the Lord. Look at the following verses and underline those phrases and words about God that can motivate and inspire your own praise:

"For You light my lamp: The LORD my God illumines my darkness. For by You I can run upon a troop; and by my God I can leap over a wall" (Psalm 18:28-29).

"Lord, You have been our dwelling place in all generations. Before the mountains were born or You gave birth to the earth and the world, even from everlasting to everlasting, You are God" (Psalm 90:1-2).

"Praise the LORD! I will give thanks to the LORD with all my heart, in the company of the upright and in the assembly. Great are the works of the LORD; they are studied by all who delight in them. Splendid and majestic is His work, and His righteousness endures forever. He has made His wonders to be remembered; the LORD is gracious and compassionate" (Psalm 111:1-4).

ADORE GOD IN PRAYER

Take some time now and turn to your prayer pages in the back of this book and devote a page to praise for your Lord. This may be especially challenging if you are experiencing a difficult circumstance in your life. You may even want to use some of the verses of praise you have read today in your time of praise.

YIELD YOURSELF TO GOD

Praise and thanksgiving are very closely akin to each other. Outwardly it is not possible to draw a clear line of demarcation between them. Both consist in giving glory to God. From ancient times, however, men have tried to differentiate between them by saying that when we give thanks, we give God the glory for what He has done for us; and when we worship or give praise, we give God glory for what He is in Himself. In that event, praise lies upon a higher plane than thanksgiving. When

I give thanks, my thoughts still circle about myself to some extent. But in praise my soul ascends to self-forgetting adoration, seeing and praising only the majesty and power of God, His grace and redemption.[6]

OLE HALLESBY

The true comprehension of God's greatness will take time. But if our faith grows strong in the knowledge of what a great and powerful God we have, we will be compelled to worship before this great and mighty God.[7]

ANDREW MURRAY

ENJOY HIS PRESENCE

What is the most important truth you've learned about praise today? Close your time with the Lord using the words of Asaph: "You are glorious and more majestic than the everlasting mountains" (Psalm 76:4 NLT). Think throughout the day about the glory and excellence of your mighty Lord.

REST IN HIS LOVE

"Whom have I in heaven but You? And besides You, I desire nothing on earth" (Psalm 73:25).

PRESUMING GOD'S CARE AND COMPASSION

But certainly God has heard;
He has given heed to the voice of my prayer.
Blessed be God, who has not turned away my prayer
Nor His lovingkindness from me.
PSALM 66:19-20

PREPARE YOUR HEART

The psalms are filled with prayers, and behind this fact is a very important presumption on the part of the psalmists; God cares for them and hears their prayers. This presumption is not a guess or even a hope on their part and is certainly not presumptuous in the negative sense. Rather, it is their exercise of faith in the facts of God as revealed in His Word. The psalmists cry out because they know He hears and will answer in His time and in His way. They have learned that sometimes a prayer requires patient waiting for the perfect timing of God. Their eyes are fixed on their God, and their hearts are steadfast as they anticipate and eagerly watch for what He will do. Have you learned this secret as it is demonstrated in the lives of the psalmists? Today, ask God to open your eyes and quiet your heart as you draw near to Him.

READ AND STUDY GOD'S WORD

1. Some of the psalms have no author's name attached and are called "orphan psalms." Even though an author is not named, much can be discovered about the circumstances of the psalmist simply by reading the psalm. Today you are going to spend some time in one of these psalms. Turn to Psalm 66 and read the words of this psalmist, writing out everything you notice about his life experience.

2. This psalmist has experienced testing, refining, and affliction that felt like a fiery trial

(Psalm 66:10-12). But notice that the Lord brought this blessed soul through the fire to a "place of abundance" (Psalm 66:12). And through it all, this one was convinced that the Lord heard his prayers and answered (Psalm 66:19). Over and over again, the psalmists declare the faithfulness, care, and concern of God in hearing and answering their prayers. Read the following verses and underline your favorite phrases and words. As you read, talk with the Lord, thanking Him for how He hears and answers your prayers.

> "But know that the LORD has set apart the godly man for Himself; the LORD hears when I call to Him" (Psalm 4:3).

> "In my distress I called upon the LORD, and cried to my God for help; He heard my voice out of His temple, and my cry for help before Him came into His ears" (Psalm 18:6).

> "The righteous cry, and the LORD hears and delivers them out of all their troubles. The LORD is near to the brokenhearted and saves those who are crushed in spirit" (Psalm 34:17-18).

> "I waited patiently for the LORD; and He inclined to me and heard my cry" (Psalm 40:1).

ADORE GOD IN PRAYER

Thank You, Lord, that You always listen, hear my prayer, and pour Your love out on me.

YIELD YOURSELF TO GOD

Here is a part in the program of God's dealings, a secret chamber of isolation in prayer and faith which every soul must enter that is very fruitful. There are times and places where God will form a mysterious wall around us, and cut away all props, and all the ordinary ways of doing things, and shut us up to something divine, which is utterly new and unexpected, something that old circumstances do not fit into, where we do not know just what will happen, where God is cutting the cloth of our lives on a new pattern, where He makes us look to Himself. Most religious people live in a sort of treadmill life, where they can calculate almost everything that will happen, but the souls that God leads out into immediate and special dealings, He shuts in where all they know is that God has hold of them, and is dealing with them, and their expectation is from Him alone...we must be detached from outward things and attached inwardly to the Lord alone in order to see His wonders.[8]

GEORGE WATSON

ENJOY HIS PRESENCE

Perhaps you are in the place George Watson described, and God is cutting the cloth of your life on a new pattern. You can confidently call out to the Lord, trusting Him to bring you into a wide and spacious place of abundance.

How have you seen the Lord hear and answer your prayers? Close your time by thanking God for specific ways He has answered your prayers.

REST IN HIS LOVE

"You made men ride over our heads; we went through fire and through water, yet You brought us out into a place of abundance" (Psalm 66:12).

PERSONALIZING GOD'S PRESENCE

You are my King, O God.
PSALM 44:4

PREPARE YOUR HEART

Why did the psalmists have such a vibrant relationship with God? They developed the habit of personalizing what they learned about God, applying it to their own lives. To the sons of Korah, who wrote Psalm 44, God was not only King, but *their* King. This is such a great secret to experiencing the power of prayer—getting personal with God. Learn to personalize each phrase, each word in the Bible for your life. When you do, your heart will catch on fire for the Lord. In fact, you will discover that the Word is indeed like fire, as the Lord told Jeremiah (Jeremiah 23:29). Personalizing the Word will help make it the joy and delight of your heart as it was for Jeremiah (Jeremiah 15:16). Draw near to God now and ask Him to speak to you from His Word today.

READ AND STUDY GOD'S WORD

1. The sons of Korah wrote some of the psalms. They were the Levitical choir made up of the descendants of Korah appointed by David to serve in the ministry of the temple. Twelve of the psalms are ascribed to the sons of Korah (Psalms 42–49; 84–85; 87–88).

Look at the following verses and write out what you learn about God in these verses. Note how the sons of Korah personalized these truths about God in their own lives.

Psalm 42:8-9

Psalm 43:4

Psalm 44:4

Psalm 46:1

Psalm 46:7

Psalm 48:9-14

Psalm 88:1-2

2. What is your favorite truth about God you learned in your time in His Word, and how can you personalize it in your own life today?

ADORE GOD IN PRAYER

> Our Father, delight Thy children with Thy presence. Indulge us with Thy smile. For a little longer we are spared in this vale of tears; but soon we hope to see Thy face behind the curtain, in the land of the blessed, in the home of Thy people. Till then, refresh our waiting spirits. Give us drops of heaven's glory before we come to bathe our souls in it. Refresh us with heaven's manna before we sit at the heavenly table.[9]
>
> CHARLES SPURGEON

YIELD YOURSELF TO GOD

> The Psalms are acts of obedience, answering the God who has addressed us... These responses are often ones of surprise, for who expects God to come looking for us? And they are sometimes awkward, for in our religious striving we are usually looking for something quite other than the God who has come looking for us. God comes and speaks—his word catches us in sin, finds us in despair, invades

us by grace. The Psalms are our answers. We don't always like what God speaks to us, and we don't always understand it…But what is critical is that we speak to the God who speaks to us, and to everything that he speaks to us, and in our speaking (which gathers up our listening and answering) mature in the great art of conversation with God that is prayer. The Psalms—all of which listen in order to answer—train us in the conversation.[10]

EUGENE PETERSON

ENJOY HIS PRESENCE

Think about your relationship with God. How personal are you with God? Have you opened up your heart to walk and talk with Him in the everyday events of your life? Ole Hallesby writes about this:

He desires to share with you the little things of life. That is always the way when two people love each other. They share everything, little things as well as big things, their joys as well as their sorrows. That is what makes love so rich and so joyous. Speak, therefore, with God about your daily experiences.[11]

In other words, get personal with God and pour out your heart. When you do, you will discover the delight of His presence. Hallesby describes the beauty of God's presence:

Nothing is so blessed as quiet, unbroken communication with our Lord. The sense of the Lord's nearness, which fills our souls, is greater than any other peace, joy, inner satisfaction, or security which we have known. Even adversity and sorrow lose their sting when we share everything with the Lord.[12]

May you know His presence in deeper and more meaningful ways with each passing day.

A little while with Jesus—
Oh, how it soothes the soul,
And gathers all the threads of life
Into a perfect whole.[13]

REST IN HIS LOVE

"We pondered your love-in-action, God, waiting in your temple: Your name, God, evokes a train of Hallelujahs wherever It is spoken, near and far; your arms are heaped with goodness-in-action. Be glad, Zion Mountain; Dance, Judah's daughters! He does what he said he'd do! Circle Zion, take her measure, count her fortress peaks, gaze long at her sloping bulwark, climb her citadel heights—then you can tell the next generation detail by detail the story of God, our God forever, who guides us till the end of time" (Psalm 48:9-14 MSG).

DEVOTIONAL READING
BY EUGENE PETERSON

God works with words. He uses them to make a story of salvation. He pulls us into the story. When we believe, we become willing participants in the plot. We can do this reluctantly and minimally, going through the motions; or we can do it recklessly and robustly, throwing ourselves into the relationships and actions. When we do this, we pray. We practice the words and phrases that make us fluent in the conversation that is at the center of the story. We develop the free responses that answer to the creating word of God in and around us that is making a salvation story...When we pray we can no longer confine our understanding of ourselves to who we are or have been; we understand ourselves in terms of possibilities yet to be realized—in St. Paul's phrase, "the glory yet to be revealed"...

The end of prayer, all prayer, is praise. Our lives fill out in goodness; earth and heaven meet in an extraordinary conjunction. Clashing cymbals announce the glory: Blessing. Amen. Hallelujah.[14]

Take some time now to write about all that you have learned this week. What has been most significant to you? Close by writing a prayer to the Lord.

PRAYER WHEN YOU
WANT TO ADORE GOD

PSALM 104

More than any other single book, Biblical or otherwise, the book of Psalms teaches us how to worship. Each psalm expresses, not merely the heart of the composer, but also the heart of the Holy Spirit Who inspired the composition. The more we read, study, meditate upon, sing and pray the psalms, the more we will worship with authenticity and ardor. The psalms invite us to go deeper with the Lord than we have gone before—and they expand the horizons of our heart for God as well.

THE NIV WORSHIP BIBLE

BLESSING THE LORD

Bless the LORD, O my soul!
PSALM 104:1

PREPARE YOUR HEART

Isaac Watts was born on July 17, 1674, in Southampton and was the oldest of nine children. His father was deacon of the Congregational chapel in Southampton. Music in the church at this time consisted of "odd versions of the Psalms." Hymns were rarely used in public worship in England. Isaac Watts, only 18 at the time, could hardly bear to hear the music and complained bitterly to his father that it sounded like a rusty saw being sharpened close to his ear.

His father sharply replied, "Then give us something better, young man!"

Well, the young man did, and that very night, the evening service in the chapel was closed with a new hymn. Isaac Watts wrote the words, based on Revelation 5:6-12: "Behold the Glories of the Lamb." From that day on, Watts poured forth a plethora of sacred poetry, bringing a fresh hymn text each Sunday to the chapel until he produced almost an entire volume.

He preached his first sermon at the age of 24 but was forced to retire from regular pastoral work due to ill health. He lived with friends, Sir Thomas and Lady Abney, in Hertfordshire for 36 years. He was a loved and honored guest—free to write, visit friends, or preach when his health permitted. This poet-preacher lived and worked in well-arranged rooms. On his table lay his lute, a telescope, books, and his Bible. He wrote hundreds of hymn texts, and some have become the favorites of many people, including "When I Survey the Wondrous Cross" and "O God, Our Help in Ages Past." One writer describes Watts, saying, "His great desire was to be of help to the worshipper in drawing near to God. He tried to express the breathings and aspirations of the Christian soul; its love, its fears, its hopes, its faith, its wonder, its sorrow, and its joy, and to lead it to sing the praises of God with understanding."[1] Isaac Watts, in his own words, points out his own goal with his writings—to bless the Lord. His audience was the Lord Himself. He said, "I make no pretence to be a poet, but to the Lamb that was once slain, and now lives, I have addressed many a song, to be sung by the penitent and believing heart."[2] A.W. Tozer, beloved preacher and writer, sang the praises of the hymns of Isaac Watts. He said, "After the Bible the next most valuable book for the Christian is a good hymnal. Let any young Christian spend a year prayerfully meditating on the hymns of Watts and Wesley alone and he will become a fine theologian."[3]

Adoring God is your first prayer and your best prayer. Your adoration is the foundation of passionate prayer, and it brings blessing to the heart of God. Just imagine making God smile—that's really what it means to bless the Lord. One smile from Him changes the whole landscape of your being and existence. Today as you draw near to God, ask Him to speak to you from His Word and show you in a new and deeper way the meaning of adoration and praise.

Begin your quiet time today by meditating on and praying the words from the stanza of Isaac Watts' first hymn:

> Behold the glories of the Lamb
> Amidst His Father's throne.
> Prepare new honors for His Name,
> And songs before unknown.

READ AND STUDY GOD'S WORD

1. Today you are going to begin a journey across the landscape of Psalm 104, a meditation on the greatness and glory of God. And what is the purpose? To bless the Lord. In fact, you might consider Psalm 104 a call to your soul to praise your Lord. At the beginning of this psalm, the psalmist says, "Bless the LORD, O my soul!" And in concluding, he says, "Let my meditation be pleasing to Him."

Read Psalm 104:1-34 and write out your favorite verse.

2. Blessing the Lord was a resolve and a commitment in the hearts of the psalmists. Look at the following verses and underline your favorite words and phrases:

> "I will bless the LORD who has counseled me; indeed, my mind instructs me in the night. I have set the LORD continually before me; because He is at my right hand, I will not be shaken. Therefore my heart is glad and my glory rejoices; my flesh also will dwell securely" (Psalm 16:7-9).

> "I will bless the LORD at all times; His praise shall continually be in my mouth" (Psalm 34:1).

"Bless the LORD, O my soul, and all that is within me, bless His holy name. Bless the LORD, O my soul, and forget none of His benefits; who pardons all your iniquities, who heals all your diseases; who redeems your life from the pit, who crowns you with lovingkindness and compassion; who satisfies your years with good things, so that your youth is renewed like the eagle" (Psalm 103:1-5).

"But as for us, we will bless the LORD from this time forth and forever. Praise the LORD!" (Psalm 115:18).

ADORE GOD IN PRAYER

We sing the greatness of our God that made the mountains rise,
That spread the flowing seas abroad and built the lofty skies.
We sing the wisdom that ordained the sun to rule the day;
The moon shines full at His command, and all the stars obey.

We sing the goodness of the Lord that filled the earth with food;
He formed the creatures with His word and then pronounced them good.
Lord, how Thy wonders are displayed where'er we turn our eyes;
In every season of the year, and through the changing skies.

There's not a plant or flower below but makes Thy glories known;
And clouds arise and tempests blow by order from Thy throne,
While all that borrows life from Thee is ever in Thy care,
And everywhere that man can be, Thou, God, art present there.

ISAAC WATTS

YIELD YOURSELF TO GOD

This lyrical poem of the whole universe—the heavens and the earth—rightly called an inspired Oratorio of Creation, instructs us how to admire with one eye the works of God, and with the other, God Himself their Creator and Preserver. Such a solemn and exalted poetic portrayal of the Cosmos in brief compass yet comprehensive and sublime has never been surpassed.[5]

HERBERT LOCKYER

ENJOY HIS PRESENCE

Will you resolve today to allow your soul to soar the heights of spiritual adventure and bless the Lord? Sometimes this is a great articulation of faith, for the darkness of a trial may blind the physical eyes, and yet such praise and adoration enable the eyes of your heart to venture into the very portals of heaven (see Ephesians 1:18-23). What is one blessing you can praise the Lord for today? Close your quiet time with your praise and adoration.

REST IN HIS LOVE

"But as for us, we will bless the LORD from this time forth and forever. Praise the LORD!" (Psalm 115:18).

FOR WHO HE IS

O LORD my God, You are very great;
You are clothed with splendor and majesty.

PSALM 104:1

PREPARE YOUR HEART

God is always more than you know Him to be right now, for He is infinite, eternal, and uncreated. Try wrapping your mind around the person of God, and you will find yourself silenced in reverence and awe. But then, as your eyes are opened to the radiance of His beauty and the majesty of His glory, you will wish, as Charles Wesley did, for a thousand tongues to praise Him. No wonder Isaac Watts was never lacking for words in the hymns he wrote. The Bible was his source of inspiration. And the Bible is your source as well. Begin your time meditating on the words of David in Psalm 103.

READ AND STUDY GOD'S WORD

1. As you continue your time in Psalm 104, read verse 1 and write it out word-for-word in the space provided, praying the words as you write.

2. In Psalm 104:1, the psalmist says, "O LORD, my God, You are very great." Note the personal nature of this phrase. He is the God *I* worship. He is *my* God.

The Hebrew word translated "great" is *gadal* and means to magnify and consider important and powerful. Here the psalmist is focusing on the omnipotence, the all-powerful nature of God. And in the psalmist's words, we learn something practical for our own conversation with God. We need to slow down to take time to praise God for who He is. Therefore, it is essential that we know who He is. He has revealed Himself through His names, His attributes, His works, and His words. You can discover His revelation generally in creation and specifically in the Word of God. Whenever you read a passage of Scripture, always look for truths God is revealing to you about Himself. The more you know, the more you can praise.

Read Psalm 31 and write out everything you learn about God.

3. Think about your own relationship with the Lord. What has God shown you about Himself so far in your adventure with Him? Write it out in the space provided.

ADORE GOD IN PRAYER

Take some time now and praise and adore God for all that He has shown you about Himself. You might read through what you just wrote in the Read and Study God's Word section of your quiet time—what you have learned from God in His Word is fuel for dynamic praise and worship of God. Pray the following prayer by Isaac Watts in order to, as he says, "abase us before the throne of God, to awaken our reverence, our dependence, our faith and hope, our humility, and joy":

> Thou art very great, O Lord, thou art clothed with honour and majesty. Thou art the blessed and only potentate, king of kings, and lord of lords. All things are naked and open before thine eyes. Thou searchest the heart of man, but how unsearchable is thine understanding, and thy power is unknown. Thou art of purer eyes than to behold iniquity. Thy mercy endureth forever. Thou art slow to anger, abundant in goodness, and thy truth reaches to all generations.[5]

YIELD YOURSELF TO GOD

> From the effort to understand, we must not turn back because the way is difficult and there are no mechanical aids for the ascent. The view is better farther up and the journey is not one for the feet but for the heart. Let us seek, therefore, such "trances of thought and mountings of the mind" as God may be pleased to grant us, knowing that the Lord often pours eyesight on the blind and whispers to babes and sucklings truths never dreamed of by the wise and prudent. Now the blind must see and the deaf hear. Now we must expect to receive the treasures of darkness and the hidden riches of secret places.[6]
>
> A.W. TOZER

I am so absolutely certain that coming to know Him as He really is will bring unfailing comfort and peace to every troubled heart that I long unspeakably to help everyone within my reach to this knowledge...Our Lord in His last recorded prayer said: "This is life eternal, that they might know thee, the only true God, and Jesus Christ whom thou hast sent." It is not a question of acquaintance with ourselves, or of knowing what we are, or what we do, or what we feel; it is simply and only a question of becoming acquainted with God, and getting to know what He is, and what He does, and what He feels. Comfort and peace can never come from anything we know about ourselves, but only and always from what we know about Him. We may spend our days in what we call our religious duties, and we may fill our devotions with fervor, and still may be miserable. Nothing can set our hearts at rest but a real acquaintance with God; for, after all, everything in our salvation must depend upon Him in the last instance; and, according as He is worthy or not of our confidence, so must necessarily be our comfort. If we were planning to take a dangerous voyage, our first question would be as to the sort of captain we were to have. Our common sense would tell us that if the captain were untrustworthy, no amount of trustworthiness on our part would make the voyage safe; and it would be his character and not our own that would be the thing of paramount importance to us.[7]

HANNAH WHITALL SMITH

ENJOY HIS PRESENCE

Think about these words by Tozer and Smith. What separated the psalmists from so many others is that they knew their God. Therefore, their focus was God, and their hearts were filled with praise. The more you know your God and walk and talk with Him each day, the more you will praise His name. Close your quiet time today by writing a prayer to your Lord, expressing your desire to know Him and to love Him.

REST IN HIS LOVE

"Bless the LORD, O my soul, and all that is within me, bless His holy name" (Psalm 103:1).

FOR WHAT HE DOES

O LORD, how many are Your works!
In wisdom You have made them all;
The earth is full of Your possessions.
PSALM 104:24

PREPARE YOUR HEART

Your praise and adoration of God multiplies as you see Him at work in the world and, more personally, in your own life. Jeremiah gained a new trust in God by focusing on His creation of the heavens and the earth, "Ah Lord GOD! Behold, You have made the heavens and the earth by Your great power and by Your outstretched arm!" (Jeremiah 32:17). He concluded, "Nothing is too difficult for You." Do you need a new trust in God today? Then focus your attention to the works and the omnipotent power of God. You will find that your difficulty looks different when seen through eyes beholding the manifold beauty of God. The more you see what God *has* done and what He *can* do, the more you can trust Him for what He *will* do in your life. Ask God now to open your eyes that you may behold wonderful things in His Word (Psalm 119:18). As you begin your quiet time, meditate on the words of this hymn by Isaac Watts:

> O God, our help in ages past, our hope for years to come,
> Our shelter from the stormy blast, and our eternal home.
>
> Under the shadow of Thy throne Thy saints have dwelt secure;
> Sufficient is Thine arm alone, and our defense is sure.
>
> Before the hills in order stood or earth received her frame,
> From everlasting Thou art God, to endless years the same.
>
> Thy Word commands our flesh to dust, "Return, ye sons of men:"
> All nations rose from earth at first and turn to earth again.
>
> A thousand ages in Thy sight are like an evening gone;
> Short as the watch that ends the night before the rising sun.

The busy tribes of flesh and blood, with all their lives and cares,
Are carried downward by the flood and lost in following years.

Time, like an ever rolling stream, bears all its sons away;
They fly, forgotten, as a dream dies at the opening day.

Like flowery fields the nations stand pleased with the morning light;
The flowers beneath the mower's hand lie withering ere 'tis night.

O God, our help in ages past, our hope for years to come,
Be Thou our guard while troubles last, and our eternal home.

READ AND STUDY GOD'S WORD

1. You have been taking a journey into the landscape of Psalm 104 to learn more about how to praise and adore God with a psalmist who clearly knew what to say to God. And you've noticed that he focused on the character and works of God. Today, you are going to have the opportunity to discover how the psalmist "slowed down" to think about and meditate on the works of God. Henry Law points out that "the devout mind finds rich repast in reading nature's volume. The construction of the world is a large field for thought to traverse. The firmament claims foremost admiration."[8] Now you will have the opportunity to "read nature's volume" with your own heart and "traverse" God's work in the world with your own mind. Read Psalm 104:2-30 and write out everything you learn about God.

2. What truth about God is most significant to you today and why?

ADORE GOD IN PRAYER

Notice Psalm 104:2-30 seems to move from prayers directed *to* God to declarations *about* God. However, what you discover about God in these verses can be used as subjects and meditations for your prayers. Pray through these verses, addressing the Lord with each thought that the psalmist makes about Him. For example, "Lord, You lay the beams of Your upper chambers in the waters; You make the clouds Your chariot; You walk upon the wings of the wind" (verse 3). Take time to allow your mind to focus on each attribute and ability of God as you talk with Him.

YIELD YOURSELF TO GOD

Omnipotence is not a name given to the sum of all power, but an attribute of a personal God whom we Christians believe to be the Father of our Lord Jesus Christ and of all who believe on Him to life eternal. The worshiping man finds this knowledge a source of wonderful strength for his inner life. His faith rises to take the great leap upward into the fellowship of Him who can do whatever He wills to do, for whom nothing is hard or difficult because He possesses power absolute. Since He has at His command all the power in the universe, the Lord God omnipotent can do anything as easily as anything else. All His acts are done without effort. He expends no energy that must be replenished. His self-sufficiency makes it unnecessary for Him to look outside of Himself for a renewal of strength. All the power required to do all that He wills to do lies in undiminished fullness in His own infinite being.[9]

A.W. TOZER

When we consider his nature, we stand afar off from him as creatures from a God, for he is infinitely superior to us. When we speak of his attributes a great acquaintance seems to grow between God and us, while we tell him that we have learned something of his power, his wisdom, his justice and his mercy. But when we proceed to mention the many works of his hands, by which he has tangibly revealed himself to our understanding, we seem to approach yet nearer to God.[10]

ISAAC WATTS

ENJOY HIS PRESENCE

Where in your life do you need a great trust in the Lord? How has focusing on what God has done in creating the heavens and the earth helped you trust Him more? How does focusing on His power and greatness help you praise Him more? Write your thoughts in your journal in the back of this book.

REST IN HIS LOVE

"Ah Lord God! Behold, You have made the heavens and the earth by Your great power and by Your outstretched arm! Nothing is too difficult for You" (Jeremiah 32:17).

FOR HIS ETERNAL GLORY

Let the glory of the LORD endure forever;
Let the LORD be glad in His works.

PSALM 104:31

PREPARE YOUR HEART

Have you ever stood on a mountain and gasped at the magnificence of the view from the top? Have you ever gazed at the majesty of a sunset as the red, yellow, orange, blue, purple, and black blend together in a kaleidoscope of color? Have you ever wondered at the intricacy of a rose or the beauty of a fresh snowfall? All these experiences speak of something no man or woman can escape—the eternal glory of God. God has painted the heavens and the earth with His glory. As David said in Psalm 19:1, "The heavens are telling of the glory of God; and their expanse is declaring the work of His hands." The Message states it this way: "God's glory is on tour in the skies." Today, as you continue to grow in your adoration of God, your focus will turn to His glory. Begin your time alone with the Lord by meditating on the words of David in Psalm 19:1-6. Ask God to quiet your heart and speak to you in His Word.

READ AND STUDY GOD'S WORD

1. Read Psalm 104:31 and write this verse out word-for-word in the space provided.

2. The glory of the Lord is the absolute splendor and reality of His presence. God's glory is seen throughout the Bible. Meditate on the following verses and record what you learn about God's glory:

Exodus 33:18-19

Exodus 40:34-35

Psalm 24:7-10

Psalm 66:1-3

Mark 13:26

2 Corinthians 3:18

2 Corinthians 4:6

Revelation 5:12

Revelation 21:23

ADORE GOD IN PRAYER

My all is now surrendered to you, my Lord; make of me as much as possible for your glory.[11]

F.B. MEYER

YIELD YOURSELF TO GOD

Scripture, indeed, makes known to us the time and manner of the creation; but the heavens themselves, although God should say nothing on the subject, proclaim loudly and distinctly enough that they have been fashioned by his hands; and this of itself abundantly suffices to bear testimony to men of his glory. As soon as we acknowledge God to be the supreme Architect, who has erected the beauteous fabric of the universe, our minds must necessarily be ravished with wonder at his infinite goodness, wisdom, and power.[12]

JOHN CALVIN

ENJOY HIS PRESENCE

Close your time today by meditating on the words of this great hymn text by Fanny Crosby. You may even want to sing it to the Lord.

To God be the glory—great things He hath done!
So loved He the world that He gave us His Son,
Who yielded His life an atonement for sin,
And opened the lifegate that all may go in.

Praise the Lord, praise the Lord, let the earth hear His voice
Praise the Lord, praise the Lord, let the people rejoice!
O come to the Father, through Jesus the Son,
And give Him the glory—great things He hath done!

REST IN HIS LOVE

"And the city has no need of the sun or of the moon to shine on it, for the glory of God has illumined it, and its lamp is the Lamb" (Revelation 21:23).

ETERNAL PRAISE AND GLADNESS

I will sing to the LORD as long as I live;
I will sing praise to my God while I have my being.
Let my meditation be pleasing to Him;
As for me, I shall be glad in the LORD.
PSALM 104:33-34

PREPARE YOUR HEART

Having meditated on the greatness and glory of God seen in His creation of the heavens and the earth, the psalmist concludes, "I will sing to the LORD as long as I live; I will sing praise to my God while I have my being. Let my meditation be pleasing to Him; As for me, I shall be glad in the LORD." These words are a tremendous declaration of faith and trust. Such words are easy to shout when the day is bright, but they are difficult to even whisper in the darkness of night, when the trial is prolonged.

Darlene Zschech was twelve weeks pregnant and preparing to go on a three week worship tour in the United States. She and her husband visited the obstetrician just prior to leaving on their trip. They were given the shattering news that the baby had just died in her womb. Darlene was crushed over the loss of their child. They had taken separate cars to the doctor, so she had to drive back to the house alone. She describes her experience:

> I got in the car, and I just didn't know what to think or do. I felt the depth of my sadness would become too heavy to bear. Then I heard the Holy Spirit whisper, "*Sing.*" In that moment it was the absolute last thing I wanted to do. *Sing?* I couldn't thing of anything I felt less like doing. But again I heard the Holy Spirit say, "*Sing.*" So after years of learning it is much better to obey quickly, I started to sing. My head didn't sing, and I do not even know if my heart sang, but my soul sang. It was almost involuntary.[13]

She sang a hymn first, "How Great Thou Art," and then a song she had written years before, "I Will Bless You, Lord." She describes what happened next:

By the time I got home something had definitely transpired in the spiritual realm. I had spoken many times on the power of worshiping through a trial. I had done this myself in varying degrees, but never before had I experienced the power of God so sovereignly fulfilling His promise to "heal the brokenhearted and bind up their wounds" (Psalm 147:3). The sweet presence of our glorious Savior placed me on the way to personal healing and victory.

Perhaps as you read about Darlene's experience, you are thinking about your own difficulty, and you can't imagine how you could ever sing. You may even be thinking you will never know the smile arising from a heart of gladness. Friend, the psalmist has made his declaration as a result of a prolonged meditation—long, deep thought with God—focused on the greatness and majesty of God. And somehow, he has been moved to a resolve—"I shall be glad in the LORD." Notice he doesn't just say, "I shall be glad," but "glad in the LORD."

Make it a steady habit to look long and hard at who God is, what God does, and what He says. When you do, you will find your heart moved to praise and adoration of your God regardless of the darkness that troubles your life. Always remember the promise from God of the treasures of darkness. He says, "I will give you the treasures of darkness and hidden wealth of secret places, so that you may know that it is I, the LORD, the God of Israel, who calls you by your name" (Isaiah 45:3).

The promises of God cannot be touched or changed by the troubles of life—they are unshakeable and true. And you can count on them. The great promise of God is that those who know Jesus Christ and have experienced forgiveness of sins, they possess eternal life, and they will reign forever and ever (Revelation 22:5). With eternity in view, you can sing. May the Lord give you the strength and power to sing and be glad in Him today.

READ AND STUDY GOD'S WORD

1. Read Psalm 104:33-34 and write out the phrase or word that is most significant to you today.

2. The psalmists often talk about their song to the Lord. Read the following verses and record what you learn about your song:

Psalm 13:6

Psalm 28:7

Psalm 32:7

Psalm 40:3

Psalm 96:1-4

Psalm 98:1

3. What song is the Lord giving to you right now? What is He teaching you as you are traveling with your prayer partners, the psalmists?

ADORE GOD IN PRAYER

Turn to your journal in the back of this book and write a prayer to the Lord, expressing all that is on your heart today.

YIELD YOURSELF TO GOD

Here the Psalmist points out to others their duty by his own example, declaring, that throughout the whole course of his life he will proclaim the praise of God without ever growing weary of that exercise. The only boundary which he fixes to the celebration of God's praises is death; not that the saints, when they pass from this world into another state of existence, desist from this religious duty, but because the end for which we are created is, that the divine name may be celebrated by us on the earth.[14]

JOHN CALVIN

ENJOY HIS PRESENCE

An elderly missionary lay in bed moments from stepping from time into eternity, where she would be face-to-face with her Lord. She was surrounded by her nine children, all committed to the Lord and serving Him in ministry. Suddenly, one of the children thought they heard their mother speak. The son leaned down and said, "Mother, what do you want?"

She struggled to find the strength to say one word: "Bring."

The son leaned in closer, "Mother, what do you want—we'll bring you whatever it is you want. You name it."

She said the word again, but with more authority, "Bring!" Just as her son was about to question her again, she cried even louder, "Bring!"

By now, the son, frustrated with his own desire to give his mother whatever she wanted, said again, "Mother, what is it that you want?"

Suddenly (and remarkably), his mother sat up with supernatural energy, stretched her hand toward heaven, and exclaimed, "Bring forth the royal diadem, and crown Him Lord of all!" She then leaned back on her pillow, closed her eyes, and stepped into eternity. Even near death, this blessed woman had received a song to sing to her Lord.

If she could sing then, surely we can sing now. And what will be the words of our song? We hold the words in our hands when we hold our Bible. Just open to any passage of Scripture, think on what God says, and allow His Words to dwell richly in you (Colossians 3:16). You will find His words forming a song, enabling you to sing and make melody in your heart to the Lord (Ephesians 5:19). Close your time today by thanking the Lord for the song He is placing even now in your heart.

> All hail the power of Jesus' name! Let angels prostrate fall;
> Bring forth the royal diadem, and crown Him Lord of all;
> Bring forth the royal diadem, and crown Him Lord of all.

REST IN HIS LOVE

"He put a new song in my mouth, a song of praise to our God; many will see and fear and will trust in the LORD" (Psalm 40:3).

DEVOTIONAL READING
BY ANDREW MURRAY

In prayer, God must be first. To this end, there must be secret prayer, where God and you can meet in private. The first thing must be to bow in lowly reverence before God in His glory, the Father whose name is to be hallowed, and so offer Him your adoration and worship. When you have secured some sense of His presence, you may utter your petitions in the hope, in the assurance, that He hears and accepts them and in due time will send you His answer. Above all, we have felt the need for the unceasing repetition of the loving message: take time. Give God time to reveal Himself to you. Give yourself time to be silent and quiet before Him, waiting to receive through the Spirit the assurance of His presence with you, of His power working in you. Take time to read His Word, so that from it you may know what He asks of you and what He promises you. Let the Word create around you and within you a holy atmosphere, a holy heavenly light in which your soul will be refreshed and strengthened for daily life. Yes, take time, so that God may let His holy presence enter into your heart and that your whole being may be permeated with the life and love of heaven.[15]

Take some time now to write about all that you have learned this week. How do these truths help you to adore God? What has been most significant to you? Close by writing a prayer to the Lord.

PRAYER WHEN YOU NEED TO CONFESS SIN

PSALM 51

O Christian, if you are seeking to have fellowship with Jesus, do not fear to confess each sin in the confident assurance that there is deliverance. Let there be a mutual understanding between the Lord Jesus and yourself that you will confess each sin and will obtain forgiveness. Then you will know your Lord as Jesus, who saves His people from their sins (Matthew 1:21). Believe that there is great power in the confession of sin, for the burden of sin was borne by our Lord and Savior.

ANDREW MURRAY

THE GROUND OF YOUR FORGIVENESS

Be gracious to me, O God, according to Your lovingkindness;
According to the greatness of Your compassion blot out my transgressions.

PSALM 51:1

PREPARE YOUR HEART

When you gaze at the greatness of God, your awareness of His majesty grows. You then become more and more overwhelmed with your own smallness. Spurgeon refers to this:

> There is something exceedingly improving to the mind in a contemplation of the Divinity. It is a subject so vast, that all our thoughts are lost in its immensity; so deep, that our pride is drowned in its infinity…No subject of contemplation will tend more to humble the mind, than thoughts of God.[1]

Knowing God not only humbles you but also makes you aware of any sin in your life. If you are maintaining a distance from God, if you've become so busy you hardly think of God, if you are dabbling in the things of the world, if you are worried or even bitter, if you refuse to forgive another, or if you've done anything out of disobedience to God, then meditating on God's greatness convicts you of your sin.

What are you to do? You must come to God on the basis of His forgiveness—His matchless grace demonstrated by the death of Jesus on the cross for your sins. He so loved the world that He gave His Son to die in your place (John 3:16). The basis of His forgiveness is His grace—His unconditional, unmerited favor. Paul explains the ground of our forgiveness when he says, "For by grace you have been saved through faith; and that not of yourselves, it is the gift of God; not as a result of works, so that no one may boast" (Ephesians 2:8).

Today, as you draw near to God, ask Him to help you understand His grace in a new and deeper way. When you know His grace, your passion in prayer will grow, for your heart will become more tender and soft before the Lord.

READ AND STUDY GOD'S WORD

1. This week as you live in God's Word and continue your quiet time experience of passionate prayer with the psalmists as your prayer partners, you are going to explore confession of sin. The topic may seem daunting, but prepare yourself for the best news of all if you know Christ personally: You are a recipient of the matchless grace of God. You are "justified as a gift by His grace through the redemption which is in Christ Jesus" (Romans 3:24). One of your heroes when it comes to confessing sin is David, and he is going to be your prayer partner and teach you how to come before God when you have sinned. Why is he such a good prayer partner for you in confession? Because he too was declared guilty. He was caught in the terrible sins of murder and adultery. What a story it is.

Read 2 Samuel 11:1–12:14 and write your most significant observation about David's response when he realized he had sinned.

2. Psalm 51 is David's prayer in response to his realization of his sin. Once the light was turned on and he saw what he had done, he went immediately to God. Read Psalm 51:1 and write out everything you learn about God—these are the attributes David focused on in his prayer of confession.

3. Grace is the ground of your forgiveness. Read the following verses about grace and underline your favorite words and phrases.

> "For all have sinned and fall short of the glory of God, being justified as a gift by His grace through the redemption which is in Christ Jesus" (Romans 3:23-24).

> "Therefore, having been justified by faith, we have peace with God through our Lord Jesus Christ, through whom also we have obtained our introduction by faith into this grace in which we stand; and we exult in hope of the glory of God" (Romans 5:1-2).

> "He freely bestowed [grace] on us in the Beloved" (Ephesians 1:6).

> "Therefore, let us draw near with confidence to the throne of grace, so that we may receive mercy and find grace to help in time of need" (Hebrews 4:16).

ADORE GOD IN PRAYER

Wonderful grace of Jesus, greater than all my sin;
How shall my tongue describe it, where shall its praise begin?
Taking away my burden, setting my spirit free;
For the wonderful grace of Jesus reaches me.

Wonderful grace of Jesus, reaching to all the lost,
By it I have been pardoned, saved to the uttermost.
Chains have been torn asunder, giving me liberty;
For the wonderful grace of Jesus reaches me.

Wonderful grace of Jesus, reaching the most defiled,
By its transforming power making him God's dear child,
Purchasing peace and heaven, for all eternity;
And the wonderful grace of Jesus reaches me.

Wonderful the matchless grace of Jesus, deeper than the mighty rolling sea;
Wonderful grace, all sufficient for me, for even me.
Broader than the scope of my transgressions, greater far than all my sin and shame,
O magnify the precious name of Jesus! Praise His name!

HALDOR LILLENAS

YIELD YOURSELF TO GOD

This word grace (*charis*), means the going forth in boundless oceans, according to Himself, of His mighty love, who "so loved the world that He gave His only begotten Son." The grace of God is infinite love operating by an infinite means—the sacrifice of Christ; and in infinite freedom, unhindered.[2]

WILLIAM NEWELL

God's basis must be our basis for acceptance. There is no other. We are "accepted in the beloved" (Ephesians 1:5). Our Father is fully satisfied with His beloved Son on our behalf, and there is no reason for us not to be. Our satisfaction can only spring from and rest in His satisfaction.[3]

MILES J. STANFORD

ENJOY HIS PRESENCE

Dear friend, you can be assured of the love and grace of God. Just look at the cross if you ever doubt it. We know that "God demonstrates His own love toward us, in that while we were yet sinners, Christ died for us" (Romans 5:8). Oh, what blessed words those are for the heart of anyone who is convicted of sin. God gives us gracious words. How can He say such things? Because of the cross. Jesus accomplished everything necessary to make you "accepted in the beloved." And so the throne of God is for you a throne of grace. How do you need to draw near to the throne of grace today? Write a prayer to your Lord as you close your quiet time.

REST IN HIS LOVE

"Therefore, let us draw near with confidence to the throne of grace" (Hebrews 4:16).

THE NATURE OF CONFESSION

Wash me thoroughly from my iniquity
And cleanse me from my sin.
For I know my transgressions,
And my sin is ever before me.
Against You, You only, I have sinned
And done what is evil in Your sight.

PSALM 51:2-4

PREPARE YOUR HEART

A Scottish medical doctor, W.P. Mackay, was rebellious against God from his early years on into adulthood. His mother, a godly, pious woman, wrestled in prayer for his conversion. Mackay, speaking about his rebellion, said, "Nothing made a deep impression on me. The older I grew the more wicked I became...I was in danger of becoming an infidel."

One day Mackay attended to a seriously injured laborer who was not expected to live. The man asked if someone would go to his home and get the Book. Mackay asked, "What book?"

The man replied that his landlady would know. Mackay visited the man once a day and was impressed by the quiet, peaceful expression constantly on his face. After about a week, the man died. The nurse asked, "What shall we do with this?" She held up a book.

"What book is it?" asked Mackay.

"The Bible of the poor man."

Mackay took the Bible and began looking through it. Dr. Mackay describes in his own words what happened next: "Could I trust my eyes? It was my own Bible. The Bible which my mother had given me when I left my parents' home, and which later, when short of money, I sold for a small amount. My name was still in it, written in my mother's hand. Beneath my name was the verse she had selected for me." Mackay was so overcome that through the regained possession of the Bible his mother had given him he was converted to Christ. Later, he wrote the famous hymn, "Revive Us Again."

Sometimes God will go to extreme measures to confront our rebellion and sin. He surely did in the cases of W.P. Mackay and King David. May our hearts always be tender toward God and quick to confess our sin, for then it is as though the light is turned on inside us. John tells us that "if we walk in the Light as He Himself is in the Light, we have fellowship with one another, and the blood of Jesus His Son cleanses us from all sin. If we say that we have no sin, we are deceiving ourselves and the truth is not in us. If we confess our sins, He is faithful and righteous to forgive us our sins and to cleanse us from all unrighteousness" (1 John 1:7-9).

Ask God today to wash you, cleanse you, forgive you, and cause you to stand in the Light of His presence.

READ AND STUDY GOD'S WORD

1. In day 1 you saw that the ground of David's forgiveness and your forgiveness is the grace of God. Today, read Psalm 51:2-9, the words of David's confession. What did confession involve for David?

2. Read 1 John 1:3-10. What is the great promise, and what must we do if we have sinned?

3. Confession means to agree with God that we have sinned. Norman Grubb says, "To confess is to say about my sin what God says about it. 'You say that is sin, Lord; so do I.' That is confession, of course, with the desire to be rid of the sin and the actual ceasing to do the thing, or maintain the attitude, or whatever it is." Confession restores your fellowship with the Lord and is essential for you to live in communion with God. Sin also requires repentance (Luke 24:47; Acts 2:38), meaning you make a turn away from your sinful, self-absorbed ways of life to follow Christ. Don't stay at a distance from God; run quickly and freely to His throne of grace.

As you think about confession and repentance, what sins do you need to bring to the throne of grace today and confess to your Lord? Sometimes you may feel as though your sin has piled high and you have been running from God for a long time. In this case, you might take a sheet of paper and write out everything you want to confess to God. Then write the words of 1 John 1:9 across the entire paper. Then, rip that piece of paper into a thousand pieces and throw them away. For the promise remains that "as far as the east is from the west, so far has He removed our transgressions from us" (Psalm 103:12).

Write a prayer now, thanking the Lord for His forgiveness.

ADORE GOD IN PRAYER

Pray the words of Psalm 51:2-9 for any sins in your life today:

Wash me thoroughly from my iniquity
And cleanse me from my sin.
For I know my transgressions
And my sin is ever before me.
Against You, You only, I have sinned
And done what is evil in Your sight,
So that You are justified when You speak
And blameless when You judge.

Behold, I was brought forth in iniquity,
And in sin my mother conceived me.
Behold, You desire truth in the innermost being,
And in the hidden part You will make me know wisdom.
Purify me with hyssop, and I shall be clean;
Wash me, and I shall be whiter than snow.
Make me to hear joy and gladness,
Let the bones which You have broken rejoice.
Hide Your face from my sins
And blot out all my iniquities.

YIELD YOURSELF TO GOD

Confession means not only that you confess your sin with shame, but also that you hand it over to God, trusting Him to take it away. Such a confession implies that you are wholly unable to get rid of your guilt, but by an act of faith you depend on God to deliver you. This deliverance means, in the first place, that you know your sins are forgiven, and secondly, that Christ undertakes to cleanse you from the sin and keep you from its power.[4]

ANDREW MURRAY

Repentance is more than regret or remorse. It is more than just being sorry, or apologizing to God. Repentance is deep conviction that brings a change of heart and leads to a change of behavior (reformation). A temporary change of behavior is not enough—it must be a permanent change if it is true repentance. Repentance is recognizing we are living and behaving in a way that grieves God's Spirit and then turning and changing to live the way God wants us to live. Some think that repentance has only to do with conversion. But it is more than that. Our whole Christian life must be one of ongoing repentance if we are to walk in the light with Jesus. God will continue to reveal things in our lives we must deal with and forsake—deeper and deeper levels of ingrained sin He wants to purge from us so that we may grow in holiness.[5]

IAN MALINS

ENJOY HIS PRESENCE

Larry Richards says that "when we expose sin in confession, God makes our darkness light."[6]

May He change any darkness in your life to light today. If you are reading this and have never brought your sin to the Lord and asked forgiveness, then today is the day for you to come to Him. If you have never established a relationship with the Lord and want to invite Him into your life, you can pray and ask Him now: *Lord Jesus, I need You. Thank You for dying on the cross for my sins. I ask You now to come into my life, forgive my sins, and make me the person You want me to be, in Jesus' name. Amen.*

I'm saved—for Christ has died for me,
And rose again to set me free
From ev'ry chain of sin.
His precious blood has made me white;
My darkness has been changed to light
Since Christ has entered in.

I'm satisfied!—I want no more.
My Lord supplies from His great store
The grace for all my needs.
The Bread of Life for soul is food,
His bounty gives me ev'ry good;
My prayer He always heeds.

I'm singing!—Christ is all my song;
Gone is the one I sang so long.
Now Christ alone I praise!
His character my theme shall be.
Through time and all eternity
His worth my voice shall raise![7]

P. HISCOCK

REST IN HIS LOVE

"God is Light, and in Him there is no darkness at all" (1 John 1:5).

THE JOY OF RESTORATION AND RENEWAL

Create in me a clean heart, O God,
And renew a steadfast spirit within me.
PSALM 51:10

PREPARE YOUR HEART

Nothing is so refreshing as cool water on a hot day. Imagine a spiritual spa for the soul, and you will understand what God does in washing you clean with His forgiveness and grace and mercy and love. He restores your heart and renews your spirit. Such refreshment is God's idea of a spiritual spa. In fact, Peter says, "Repent and return, so that your sins may be wiped away, in order that times of refreshing may come from the presence of the Lord" (Acts 3:19). Ask the Lord to give you a time of refreshing today.

READ AND STUDY GOD'S WORD

1. Read Psalm 51:10 and write it out word-for-word in the space provided. As you write, pray these words to your Lord.

2. Psalm 32 is also written by David and declares the joy of forgiveness. Read Psalm 32:1-11 and write out everything that David learned.

ADORE GOD IN PRAYER

Personalize these words to pray them for yourself: "Revive me again, fill my heart with your love…"

> Revive us again,
> Fill each heart with Thy love
> May each soul be rekindled
> With fire from above.
> Hallelujah! Thine the glory!
> Hallelujah! Amen!
> Hallellujah! Thine the glory!
> Revive us again.

WILLIAM MACKAY

YIELD YOURSELF TO GOD

Desire of pardon is linked to earnest longing for renewing and sanctifying grace. The cleansing of the heart is the absolute work of God. It is a new creation. It is calling that into existence which no power of man could accomplish. Conscious of utter impotency, the cry struggles for creating and renewing grace.[8]

HENRY LAW

Can we expect always to live in a state of spiritual alertness and freshness? Isn't that being unrealistically optimistic? Well, what does Scripture say? It shows that the people of God are meant to be beautiful gardens in the midst of a dry desert. The prophet Isaiah puts it like this: "And you shall be like a watered garden and like a spring of water whose waters fail not" (Isaiah 58:11 AMP)…The river of God flowing into our dead seas turns them fresh. Whatever reasons there are for our lives becoming spiritually stale, it is quite clear from Scripture that they need not be so. God offers to exchange His strength daily for our weakness, His freshness for our staleness.[9]

SELWYN HUGHES

ENJOY HIS PRESENCE

Will you become practiced in drawing near to your Lord that He may daily revive your heart? What is the most significant insight you have learned from your quiet time today? Thank the Lord for what you have learned by writing a prayer in your journal expressing all that is on your heart.

REST IN HIS LOVE

"You are my hiding place; You preserve me from trouble; You surround me with songs of deliverance" (Psalm 32:7).

THE POWER OF THE SPIRIT

Do not cast me away from Your presence
And do not take Your Holy Spirit from me.
Restore to me the joy of Your salvation
And sustain me with a willing spirit.
PSALM 51:11-12

PREPARE YOUR HEART

Once you have been cleansed from sin, you need to yield control to the indwelling Holy Spirit. When you do, you are filled (controlled and empowered) by the Spirit. He is your strength and power in every situation. When you are living in the power of the Holy Spirit, even in impossible situations you will be able to cry out, "I can't, but He can." Today ask the Lord to show you how to live in the power of the Holy Spirit.

READ AND STUDY GOD'S WORD

1. David knew he needed the power of the Holy Spirit in his life if he was to walk in victory, experience joy, and live a yielded, holy life. Read Psalm 51:11-13 and write out what is most significant to you about David's words.

2. The New Testament has much to say about the Spirit-filled life. Read these verses and record what you learn about the Holy Spirit:

Ephesians 5:18

Galatians 5:16-26

3. How will walking by the Spirit help you choose to say no to sin and yes to Christ?

ADORE GOD IN PRAYER

In what ways do you need to surrender to the power and control of the Holy Spirit today? Turn to your prayer pages and devote a page to all the areas of surrender to your Lord.

YIELD YOURSELF TO GOD

Through the Holy Spirit we may experience the love and abiding presence of the Lord Jesus throughout the day. But let us remember that the Spirit of God must have entire possession of us. He claims our hearts and our entire lives. He will strengthen us with might in the inner man (Ephesians 3:16), so that we may have fellowship with Christ, keep His commandments, and abide in His love. Once we have grasped this truth, we will begin to feel our deep dependence on the Holy Spirit and will ask the Father to send Him in power into our hearts. The Spirit will teach us to love the Word, to meditate on it, and to keep it. He will reveal the love of Christ to us, so that we may love Him "fervently with a pure heart" (1 Peter 1:22). Then we will begin to see that having the love of Christ in the midst of our daily lives and distractions is a glorious possibility and a blessed reality.[10]

ANDREW MURRAY

ENJOY HIS PRESENCE

Will you, dear friend, pray and ask God to fill you with His Holy Spirit? Yield control of your life to Him and allow Him to guide and direct you every moment of the day. When you sin, immediately confess your sin. Then pray and ask the Lord to once again fill (control and empower) you with the Holy Spirit. Nothing is so exciting as the Spirit-filled life! Jesus describes the Holy Spirit moving in your life as "rivers of living water" flowing from your innermost being (John 7:37-39). When you are led by the Spirit, you are led by Christ Himself. What an adventure it is to follow Christ. As Tozer pointed out many years ago, the Spirit-filled life is "the normal state for every redeemed man and woman the world over. It is 'that mystery which hath been hid from ages and from generations, but now is made manifest to his saints: to whom God would make known what is the riches of the glory of this mystery among the Gentiles: which is Christ in you, the hope of glory'" (Colossians 1:26 KJV).[11]

> Ocean, wide flowing Ocean, Thou,
> Of uncreated Love;
> I tremble as within my soul
> I feel Thy waters move.
> Thou art a sea without a shore;
> Awful, immense Thou art;
> A sea which can contract itself
> Within my narrow heart.

FREDERICK WILLIAM FABER

REST IN HIS LOVE

"Since we live by the Spirit, let us keep in step with the Spirit" (Galatians 5:25 NIV).

THE BEAUTY OF HUMILITY

The sacrifices of God are a broken spirit;
A broken and a contrite heart, O God, You will not despise.
PSALM 51:17

PREPARE YOUR HEART

When you have been broken and restored, a new quality begins to shine from within—humility. Oh, how beautiful is one who has a humble heart! God can use the humble man or woman in the highest and holiest of service. Don't be afraid of the way of humility. Mrs. Charles Cowman, author of *Streams in the Desert,* encourages the way of humility—what she calls the "hidden life":

> God's servants must be taught the value of the hidden life. The man who is to take a high place before his fellows must take a low place before his God. We must not be surprised if sometimes our Father says: "There, child, thou hast had enough of this hurry, and publicity, and excitement: get thee hence, and hide thyself by the brook"... Happy is he who can reply, "This Thy will is also mine; I flee unto Thee to hide me. Hide me in the secret of Thy tabernacle, and beneath the cover of Thy wings!"[12]

Today ask the Lord to show you the beauty of a humble heart.

READ AND STUDY GOD'S WORD

1. Read Psalm 51:17, the words of David as a result of his confession. What did he learn from the Lord?

2. Jesus esteemed the humble, broken heart in the parable found in Luke 18:9-14. Read this parable and record all that you notice about the tax collector. Describe his actions in detail.

3. Look at the following verses and write what you learn about humility:

Matthew 23:10-12

Philippians 2:1-11

James 4:8-10

1 Peter 5:6-7

ADORE GOD IN PRAYER

Use the words of the tax collector in the parable of Jesus as your prayer: "God, be merciful to me, the sinner" (Luke 18:13).

YIELD YOURSELF TO GOD

True humility comes when, in the light of God, we have seen ourselves to be nothing, have consented to part with and cast away self, to let God be all. The soul that has done this, and can say, So have I lost myself in finding Thee, no longer compares itself with others. It has given up forever every thought of self in God's presence; it meets its fellowmen as one who is nothing, and seeks nothing for itself; who is a servant of God, and for His sake a servant of all. A faithful servant may be wiser than the master, and yet retain the true spirit and posture of the servant... The humble man looks upon every, the feeblest and unworthiest, child of God, and honours him and prefers him in honour as the son of a King. The spirit of Him who washed the disciples' feet, makes it a joy to us to be indeed the least, to be servants of one another. The humble man feels no jealousy or envy. He can praise God when others are preferred and blessed before him. He can bear to hear others praised and himself forgotten, because in God's presence he has learnt to say with

Paul, "I am nothing." He has received the spirit of Jesus, who pleased not Himself, and sought not His own honour, as the spirit of his life.[13]

ANDREW MURRAY

ENJOY HIS PRESENCE

As you close your quiet time today, think about all you have learned this week about confession from your prayer partner, David, in Psalm 51. What is the most important truth you have learned? How will it change how you pray and walk with your Lord? Write a prayer to the Lord, expressing all that is on your heart.

REST IN HIS LOVE

"Therefore humble yourselves under the mighty hand of God, that He may exalt you at the proper time, casting all your anxiety on Him, because He cares for you" (1 Peter 5:6).

DEVOTIONAL READING
BY BRENNAN MANNING

Lord Jesus, we are silly sheep who have dared to stand before you and try to bribe you with our preposterous portfolios. Suddenly we have come to our senses. We are sorry and ask you to forgive us. Give us the grace to admit we are ragamuffins, to embrace our brokenness, to celebrate your mercy when we are at our weakest, to rely on your mercy no matter what we do. Dear Jesus, gift us to stop grandstanding and trying to get attention, to do the truth quietly without display, to let the dishonesties in our lives fade away, to accept our limitations, to cling to the gospel of grace, and to delight in your love. Amen.[14]

Take some time now to write about all that you have learned this week. What has been most significant to you? Close by writing a prayer to the Lord.

PRAYER WHEN YOU WANT TO SAY THANK YOU

PSALM 138

Having received something from God,
it is self-evident that we ought to
return thanks to Him for it.

OLE HALLESBY

THE RESOLVE OF THANKSGIVING

I will give You thanks with all my heart;
I will sing praises to You before the gods.
PSALM 138:1

PREPARE YOUR HEART

They were outcasts. Each of them had received the dreaded diagnosis—leprosy! No one wanted to get close to them. They were untouchable and had no hope of any kind of life that could be called life.

One day, the atmosphere of their village felt different. Palpable excitement was in the air! Jesus was coming, the one many said was a prophet. Word was that He actually healed people with various illnesses. And now the crowds began to gather.

One small group of men, ten to be exact, stood at a distance. They could not get close because they were lepers. Branded with something none of them could have imagined they would have. But they did—and it was fatal. They only had sorrow and suffering ahead in their lives.

But now Jesus was coming to their village. What if He could heal people? Could He do something for their disease? If they could make contact, maybe they could ask Him to help them. And so they stood, watching, waiting. They could tell He was near because the noise in the crowd got louder as many called out to Him and drew near to catch a glimpse or even touch Him. Finally, the lepers could wait no longer. They left their safe area of quarantine and bolted in the direction of the crowd. And turning the corner, there He was—Jesus, the one they had heard so much about.

"Jesus, Master, have mercy on us!" they cried. His eyes met theirs, and they felt a warmth, a kindness, a love like they had never known before.

"Go and show yourselves to the priests," He said. What? He didn't come over to them, didn't say, "Be healed." Just, "Go, show yourselves to the priests." What an outrageous suggestion! Only lepers who were healed would go to the priests.

But these ten lepers received His direction and did not stop to ask why. They turned and headed in the direction of the priests. As they were going, they looked at their skin. Their hearts began to race…the leprosy was completely gone! They ran faster, hardly able to wait to show the priests what had happened.

But one stopped while the others kept running. He just could not believe the leprosy was healed. But it was. He turned and began running the opposite direction, with only one thought on his mind—he *had* to see Jesus again. With loud shouts and praise, thanking God all the way, he turned the corner and fell at Jesus' feet. He couldn't say thank you enough. No words could express the gratitude welling up in his heart. The man was speechless.

"Were there not ten cleansed? But the nine—where are they? Was no one found who returned to give glory to God, except this foreigner?" Then Jesus gave this man His full attention. He was personal. His words meant everything. "Stand up and go; your faith has made you well."

Jesus praised the man with the thankful heart. Oh, how our gratitude blesses our Lord. Gratitude fuels the passion of your prayers. This week, you are going to have the opportunity to learn about thanksgiving from the beloved psalmist, David, the man after God's own heart. Draw near to God now and ask Him to teach you how to express gratitude for His many blessings.

READ AND STUDY GOD'S WORD

1. Psalm 138, written by David, is a psalm of thanksgiving. Take some time now to read through this psalm and write your most significant insight.

2. Read Psalm 138:1 in the following translations and underline the phrases and words that are most important to you today:

"I will give You thanks with all my heart; I will sing praises to You before the gods."

"I will confess and praise You [O God] with my whole heart; before the gods will I sing praises to You" (AMP).

"LORD, I will thank you with all my heart; I will sing to you before the gods" (NCV).

"I will praise you, O LORD, with all my heart; before the 'gods' I will sing your praise" (NIV).

"Thank you! Everything in me says 'Thank you!' Angels listen as I sing my thanks" (MSG).

3. Note the words "I will" at the beginning of Psalm 138. What is David's resolve and commitment expressed in those two words?

4. Read the event in Luke 17:11-19 describing Jesus' healing of the ten lepers. What is most significant to you?

ADORE GOD IN PRAYER

Lord, I pause to look back on the long way Thou hast brought me, on the long days in which I have been served, not according to my deserts but according to my desires and Thy loving mercies. Let me meditate upon the dark nights through which I have come, the sinister things from which I have been delivered—and have a grateful heart. Let me meditate upon my sins forgiven, for my shame unpublished—and have a grateful heart.

I thank Thee, O Lord, that, in Thy mercy, so many things I feared never came to pass. Fill my heart with thankful praise. Help me to repay in service to others the debt of Thy unmerited benefits and mercies. May the memories of sorrows that disciplined my spirit keep me humble and make me grateful that my God is no celestial Santa Claus but a divine Saviour. In His name I offer this sacrifice of praise. Amen.[1]

PETER MARSHALL

YIELD YOURSELF TO GOD

How much Jesus appreciates gratitude can be seen very clearly from the account of the ten lepers whom He restored to health (Luke 17:11-19). He had healed them by sending them to the priests to receive the certificate required by law to show that they had been cleansed of their leprosy. While they were on their way to the priests, they were suddenly cleansed, every one of them. Nine of them continued on their way to receive their certificates. And in so doing they were in reality complying with

Jesus' words, "Go and show yourselves unto the priests." One of them, however, turned about, went back to Jesus joyfully speaking His praises, fell down on his face before the Lord and returned thanks to Him. Notice the impression it made on Jesus. Listen to the tone in His query, 'Were not ten cleansed? But where are the nine? Were there none found that returned to give glory to God, save this stranger?' Here we are also told by Jesus Himself that to give thanks means to give glory to God. This explains why it is so blessed to give thanks. Even though our efforts to thank God in prayer are weak, nevertheless we find that when we succeed in truly thanking God, we feel good at heart. The reason is that we have been created to give glory to God, now and forevermore. And every time we do so, we feel that we are in harmony with His plans and purposes for our lives. Then we are truly in our element. That is why it is so blessed.[2]

OLE HALLESBY

ENJOY HIS PRESENCE

What are you most thankful for today? Draw near to the Lord like that one leper who turned back, and pour out your heart of gratitude, giving glory to God.

REST IN HIS LOVE

"He fell on his face at His feet, giving thanks to Him" (Luke 17:16).

THE REVERENCE OF THANKSGIVING

I will bow down toward Your holy temple
And give thanks to Your name for Your lovingkindness and Your truth;
For You have magnified Your word according to all Your name.

PSALM 138:2

PREPARE YOUR HEART

Your heart of reverence will lead you to thanksgiving. Reverence is your adoration and devotion to God and His Word. A devoted heart leads to a thankful heart. One of the great examples of devotion was Amy Carmichael, who left the comforts of home to live her entire life as a missionary in India. Her poetry leaves no question as to her loyalty—she was wholeheartedly devoted to her Lord.

> God of the golden dust of stars
> Scattered in space,
> God of the starry blessings that light
> Our happy place,
> God of the little things,
> We adore Thee,
> Come before Thee
> Grateful, in loving thanksgiving.
>
> God of the blue of glancing wing,
> Song of the bird,
> God of the friendly comfort of smiles,
> Cheer of a word,
> God of the little things,
> We adore Thee,
> Come before Thee
> Grateful, in loving thanksgiving.

God of the fairy pollen ball,
Frail flow'ry bell,
Touches of tenderness that would seem
Nothing to tell,
God of the little things,
We adore Thee,
Come before Thee
Grateful, in loving thanksgiving.

God of the sparkle on our day,
Gift of the sun,
Laughter that lifts, all lovely and gay,
Ripples of fun,
God of the little things,
We adore Thee,
Come before Thee
Grateful, in loving thanksgiving.[3]

AMY CARMICHAEL

READ AND STUDY GOD'S WORD

1. Read the following translations of Psalm 138:2 and underline your favorite phrases and words.

"I will bow down toward Your holy temple and give thanks to Your name for your lovingkindness and Your truth; For You have magnified Your word according to all Your name."

"I will bow down toward your holy temple and will praise your name for your love and your faithfulness, for you have exalted above all things your name and your word" (NIV).

"I will bow down facing your holy Temple, and I will thank you for your love and loyalty. You have made your name and your word greater than anything" (NCV).

"I bow before your holy Temple as I worship. I praise your name for your unfailing love and faithfulness; for your promises are backed by all the honor of your name" (NLT).

"I kneel in worship facing your holy temple and say it again: 'Thank you!' Thank you for your love, thank you for your faithfulness; most holy is your name, most holy is your Word" (MSG).

2. What is David devoted to according to his words in Psalm 138:2?

3. His devotion to God and His Word lead David to thank God. For what does he say "thank You"?

4. One of the most extravagant displays of devotion in the Bible came from the woman with the alabaster jar who anointed Jesus' feet with expensive perfume. Read Luke 7:36-50 and write out what you notice about the woman's devotion to Jesus and what her devotion meant to Jesus.

ADORE GOD IN PRAYER

How can you express your gratitude to the Lord with extravagant devotion today? Turn to your prayer pages in the back of this book and devote one page to praise and thanksgiving for the Lord's blessings in your life.

YIELD YOURSELF TO GOD

The *Oxford English Dictionary* describes *extravagant* as "wasteful." This word particularly grabbed my attention, for one of the most beautiful accounts of extravagant worship in the Bible is this story of how the gift of perfume from the sinful woman was considered "wasteful" by those around her. But as she poured out her costly perfume from the alabaster jar, she must have wished she had even more to give Him. As she poured out her tears in offering, He washed away her brokenness. As she loved extravagantly, He forgave extravagantly. Her action of elaborate love toward her Lord is a powerful example of true, heartfelt worship. Her act of worship had nothing to do with music or song, but it had all to do with being extravagant in devotion to her Savior.[4]

DARLENE ZSCHECH

ENJOY HIS PRESENCE

Your time alone with God in His Word each day is most important in developing a heart of devotion. No wonder Paul said, "Let the word of Christ dwell in you richly as you teach and admonish one another with all wisdom, and as you sing psalms, hymns, and spiritual songs with gratitude in your hearts to God" (Colossians 3:16 NIV) The Greek word translated "richly" is *plousios* and means "with extravagance." In this case, Paul is exhorting the church to be extravagant with God's Word. May the Lord bless you as you are extravagant, day by day, with God and His Word.

REST IN HIS LOVE

"Standing behind Him at His feet, weeping, she began to wet His feet with her tears, and kept wiping them with the hair of her head, and kissing His feet and anointing them with the perfume" (Luke 7:38).

THE RESPONSE TO THANKSGIVING

On the day I called, You answered me;
You made me bold with strength in my soul.
PSALM 138:3

PREPARE YOUR HEART

Cultivating a heart of thanksgiving makes us bold and courageous. No wonder David was such a champion for God. He was constantly thanking Him for the small and the great things of life. And so must we, if we are to be God's servants for such a time as this. Begin your quiet time today by meditating on one of the great psalms of thanksgiving—Psalm 100. Write out your most significant insight.

READ AND STUDY GOD'S WORD

1. Read David's words in Psalm 138:3. What was the result of his prayer and thanksgiving?

2. When you pray with thanksgiving, you receive an inner strength from the Lord. Notice that David credited the Lord for his boldness and inner strength. Look at the following verses and write out what you learn about your strength in the Lord:

Psalm 28:7-8

Psalm 37:39

Psalm 59:17

Psalm 84:5-7

Psalm 105:4

Psalm 118:14

3. Why is thanksgiving a key to experiencing the strength of the Lord?

ADORE GOD IN PRAYER

In what ways do you need the strength of the Lord today? Shower the Lord with thanksgiving for all He has done for you and ask Him for your smallest and greatest needs. Then watch eagerly to see what He will do (Psalm 5:3).

YIELD YOURSELF TO GOD

It is easy for us to think that God is so great and so highly exalted that it does not make any difference to Him whether we give thanks or not. It is, therefore, necessary for us to catch a vision of the heart of God. His is the most tender and most sensitive heart of all. Nothing is so small or inconsequential that it does not register an impression with Him, whether it be good or bad. Jesus says that He will not forget even a cup of cold water if it is given in grateful love of Him...

It is not only blessed to give thanks; it is also of vital importance to our prayer life in general. If we have noted the Lord's answers to our prayers and thanked Him for what we have received of Him, then it becomes easier for us, and we get more courage, to pray for more…

If someone has rendered a great service to you or your dear ones in a difficult situation, then you feel the desire to meet that person, grip his hand fervently and say from the bottom of your heart: "Thank you very much for what you have done for us." My friend, do the same to Jesus. He is not made of stone. He is moved to happiness every time He sees that you appreciate what He has done for you. Grip His pierced hand and say to Him, "I thank Thee, Savior, because Thou hast died for me." Thank Him likewise for all the other blessings He has showered upon you from day to day. Do this often during the day, in the midst of your work as well as when you are resting. It brings joy to Jesus. And you yourself will become glad.[5]

OLE HALLESBY

ENJOY HIS PRESENCE

Thanking the Lord changes the entire focus of your life from earth to heaven, from the temporal to the eternal. Your sights are enlarged to include the God of the impossible, Creator of the heavens and the earth, who is full of compassion and mercy. Thank the Lord today for the power of His strength and blessings in your life.

REST IN HIS LOVE

"The moment I called out, you stepped in; you made my life large with strength" (Psalm 138:3 MSG).

THE REVIVAL IN THANKSGIVING

Though I walk in the midst of trouble, You will revive me;
You will stretch forth your hand against the wrath of my enemies,
And Your right hand will save me.

PSALM 138:7

PREPARE YOUR HEART

A thankful heart is the heart that will experience personal spiritual revival. Thankfulness opens the heart up to receive what the Lord has to give. Personal revival means you are receiving day by day what you need from the Lord to be restored to God's plan and purpose for your life. Thanksgiving in your prayers encourages your revival, for it moves your eyes from yourself to God. Begin your quiet time today by asking the Lord to revive your heart. Thank Him for answering your prayer.

READ AND STUDY GOD'S WORD

1. Turn to David's words in Psalm 138:7 and write out what is most encouraging to you today.

2. Read the following words by Henry Law about Psalm 138:7 and underline what means the most to you:

> In our heavenward course troubles will beset us on the right hand and on the left. But let no fears depress us. The Lord will strengthen and refresh us. He will cause our graces to blossom like the rose. His mighty power shall be manifested in our behalf, and we shall stride victorious over all hindrances.

How have you seen the Lord refresh you in the midst of trouble and cause you to "blossom like the rose"?

3. The kind of revival spoken of in Psalm 138:7 is personal and spiritual. David says, "You will revive me." Look at the following verses and write what you learn about this kind of revival:

Psalm 69:32

Psalm 71:20

Psalm 80:17-19

Psalm 119:25

Psalm 119:50

Psalm 143:11

ADORE GOD IN PRAYER

Ask the Lord to revive your heart and refresh your spirit. You might take some extra time and write a prayer to Him in your journal in the back of this book.

YIELD YOURSELF TO GOD

Wherever there exists a cordial belief of God's truth, and submission of the will to his authority, and the graces of the heart shine forth in the virtues of the life, there is true religion; whether it be in the palace or the cottage; whether it appear in a single individual, or be diffused over a whole community. Now if such be the nature of religion, you will readily perceive in what consists a *revival* of religion. It is a revival of scriptural knowledge; of vital piety; of practical obedience…

Wherever then you see religion rising up from a state of comparative depression to a tone of increased vigor and strength; wherever you see professing Christians becoming more faithful to their obligations, and behold the strength of the church increased by fresh accessions of piety from the world; there is a state of things which you need not hesitate to denominate a revival of religion.[6]

WILLIAM B. SPRAGUE

When we come down to it in simplest form, it means *the reviving of dead areas in our lives.* I remember when I first heard two men from Ruanda speaking very quietly and simply for two days in our London WEC Headquarters to about ninety of our staff. At the last meeting, they very quietly opened the door for any present to say anything that was on their hearts. Very soon one and another were bringing to the light areas in their lives where they had come face to face with sin—unobserved by them before—and were bringing them to the cleansing blood. I got a real shock at the end when one of the two quietly said, "I don't know if you realize it friends, but this is revival!" The transforming truth of that statement took time to sink in—and is still sinking in! It began to shake me out of the misconception of years—that revival could only come in great soul-shaking outpourings of the Spirit. Thank God for such when they do come; they have been the great and precious hurricanes of the Spirit in the history of the Church. But I saw the defeatism and almost hopelessness that so many of us had fallen into by thinking that we could do nothing about revival except pray (often rather unbelievingly) and wait until the heavens rent and God came down. But now I see that "revival" in its truest sense is an everyday affair right down within the reach of everyday folk to be experienced in our hearts, homes and churches, and in our fields of service. When revival does burst forth in greater and more public ways, thank God! But meanwhile we can see to it that we are being ourselves constantly revived persons…which of course also means that others are getting revived in our own circles. By this means God can have channels of revival by the thousands in all the churches of the world![7]

NORMAN GRUBB

ENJOY HIS PRESENCE

Close your time with the Lord by describing how the Lord has revived your heart in the past and how you need revival in your life right now.

REST IN HIS LOVE

"For the sake of Your name, O LORD, revive me. In Your righteousness bring my soul out of trouble" (Psalm 143:11).

THE RELIANCE THROUGH THANKSGIVING

The LORD will accomplish what concerns me;
Your lovingkindness, O LORD, is everlasting;
Do not forsake the works of Your hands.
PSALM 138:8

PREPARE YOUR HEART

A hundred years ago, a balloonist embarked on a trip over the Alps. He planned his itinerary carefully, but each day when he approached his destination, the wind blew him in a different direction, taking him to an unplanned town. The next day, the wind carried him to another unexpected destination. Each time he landed, he said, "I didn't know about this place. Had I known, I would have planned to land here."[8] He looked at each new day as a delightful surprise rather than a disappointment. His attitude of gratitude enabled him to fly with confidence and trust.

And so it is with you. When you are thankful, you will discover you are growing confident in your trust in God. David was able to say, "The LORD will accomplish what concerns me." His words are one of the powerful promises of the Bible and are developed out of a heart of thanksgiving. If you would trust God, you must learn to thank God. *Lord, give me a thankful heart, trusting in You moment by moment throughout this day. I trust You to accomplish what concerns me.*

READ AND STUDY GOD'S WORD

1. Read Psalm 138:8 in the following translations and underline your favorite words and phrases:

> "The LORD will accomplish what concerns me; Your lovingkindness, O LORD, is everlasting; Do not forsake the works of Your hands."

> "LORD, you do everything for me. LORD, your love continues forever. Do not leave us, whom you made" (NCV).

"The LORD will fulfill his purpose for me; your love, O LORD, endures forever—do not abandon the works of your hands" (NIV).

"The Lord will perfect that which concerns me; Your mercy, O LORD, endures forever; Do not forsake the works of Your hands" (NKJV).

"The LORD will work out his plans for my life—for your faithful love, O Lord, endures forever. Don't abandon me, for you made me" (NLT).

2. The Lord desires a confident trust rather than a heart of worry. Read the following verses and record what you learn about trusting instead of worrying:

Proverbs 3:5-6

Jeremiah 17:5-8

Philippians 4:6-7

ADORE GOD IN PRAYER

Pray the words of Psalm 138 as your prayer to the Lord today.

YIELD YOURSELF TO GOD

Trust God, amid all disappointment and heartache. He will wipe away all tears, explain all mysteries, and place a pinnacle of glory on the structure of your life.

F.B. MEYER

ENJOY HIS PRESENCE

What have you learned this week that will make a difference in your life of prayer? Close by writing a prayer to the Lord in your journal, expressing all that is on your heart.

REST IN HIS LOVE

"Be anxious for nothing, but in everything by prayer and supplication with thanksgiving let your requests be made known to God. And the peace of God, which surpasses all comprehension, will guard your hearts and your minds in Christ Jesus" (Philippians 4:6-7).

DEVOTIONAL READING
BY ISAAC WATTS

To give thanks is to acknowledge the bounty of that hand from which we receive our blessings, and to ascribe honour and praise to the power, the wisdom and the goodness of God upon that account. And this is part of that tribute which God our king expects at our hands for all the favours we receive from him. It very ill-becomes a creature to partake of benefits from his God, and then to forget his heavenly benefactor and grow regardless of that bounty from which his comforts flow…

All our thanksgivings may be yet further heightened in prayer by considering the multitude of mercies that we have received, their greatness and their continuance; by mentioning the glory and self-sufficiency of God the giver: that he is happy in himself and stands in no need of us, and yet he condescends to confer perpetual benefits upon us; that he is sovereign and might dispose of his favours to thousands and leave us out of the number of his favourites. We are as vile and unworthy as others, and our God beholds all our unworthiness, all our guilt, our repeated provocations, and his past mercies abused, and yet he continues to have mercy upon us and waits to be gracious.[9]

Will you, dear friend, come reverently to God with thanksgiving in your heart? Take some time now to write about all that you have learned this week. What has been most significant to you? Close by writing a prayer to the Lord.

PRAYER WHEN YOU WANT TO ASK GOD

The way to get a thing which is purchasable is to pay for it.
The way to get a thing which is to be earned is to work for it.
The way to get a thing which is to be given is to ask for it.
The Christian in receiving from God has neither to pay nor to earn.
What he gets from God comes by gift, and the way to receive it is simply to ask.

JAMES H. McCONKEY

FOR GOD'S ANSWER

Hear my prayer, O LORD, Give ear to my supplications!
Answer me in Your faithfulness, in Your righteousness!
PSALM 143:1

PREPARE YOUR HEART

Tony Campolo was invited to speak at a college in Valley Forge, Pennsylvania. He drove to the college and met with some of the men beforehand to pray for the event. In the middle of their prayer, one of the men asked, "And Lord, about Burt Harris. Lord, Burt Harris needs you really badly. He lives in that trailer down the street and is considering leaving his wife and family. And Lord, if you could just get through to Burt Harris…that would be great." Then the man continued to pray about their upcoming event at the college.

Campolo thought, *That is strange that he should pray that here.*

Later that evening, after Campolo gave his message, he got in his car and began the journey home. He saw a hitchhiker along the side of the road. He knew he probably shouldn't pick up hitchhikers, but he felt drawn toward this man. He thought, *Being a preacher, anytime I can get a captive audience, I'll take advantage of it.* So he pulled over to let the man in his car. He began talking with him, and then he asked, "By the way, what is your name?"

"Burt Harris," the man replied.

Campolo immediately stopped the car, turned around, and drove in the opposite direction.

"What are you doing?" asked Harris.

"I'm taking you back to your wife and family, whom you are trying to leave," replied Campolo. Harris looked at him in shock. He was speechless. Campolo drove to the man's trailer.

Harris asked, "How do you know where I live?"

Campolo said, "God told me." He proceeded to take Burt Harris inside his home and talk with the family. The marriage and family were restored—all because someone was burdened for a friend and prayed. And God answered by reaching out in a very personal and miraculous way to a man whose heart was in trouble.

God will surprise you with very specific answers to your prayers when you ask Him for help for yourself and others. George Mueller saw orphans in trouble and asked God to provide the resources necessary to help them. He was so serious about his prayers that he kept a list, filling 3000 pages of his journal with all his prayer requests. His notes reveal more than 30,000 answers to his prayers.

God is serious about prayer and responds to your humble response to His invitation to ask Him for your needs. He says in James 4:2, "You do not have because you do not ask." God is waiting for you to ask Him for everything you need today. What do you need? What do you want?

King David knew the secret of always asking God first. Many people regard prayer as a last resort. But David had learned the habit of inquiring of God, seeking God, and eagerly watching and waiting for God's answer. God's answers are always better than the world's provision. A.C. Dixon, the great preacher and pastor of Chicago's famous Moody Church, declared, "When we rely upon organization, we get what organization can do; when we rely upon education, we get what education can do; when we rely upon eloquence, we get what eloquence can do. When we rely upon prayer, we get what God can do."

God has His answer for your need. How can you receive His answer? Ask Him. Today we are going to begin a week of quiet times focusing on taking our needs to God in prayer. The psalmists teach us that those who are passionate in their prayer are quick to take every need, every request to the Lord. Begin your quiet time by asking God to quiet your heart and speak to you from His Word.

READ AND STUDY GOD'S WORD

1. This week you will have the opportunity to live in Psalm 143, one of David's psalms written during a time of danger from an enemy. We are not told who the enemy is, but from David's words, we understand the enemy to be fierce enough to persecute David's soul and crush his life to the ground. Those are David's words, descriptive of a time of desperation with seemingly no earthly answer. Have you ever known a time like David's, when you had no answer? You can know that you have an answer even when you cannot see the answer. God is the answer to your need. He is not wondering what to do, and He is not worried even if you are. How did David respond when he felt crushed by his own trouble? He prayed. Read Psalm 143 and write out the prayer in this psalm that means the most to you today.

2. Psalm 143 is known in the liturgical tradition of the church as one of the seven penitential psalms of David (others are Psalms 6, 32, 38, 51, 102, and 130).[1] In each penitential psalm,

David confesses sins and asks for God's mercy and forgiveness. David does not confess specific sins in Psalm 143, but he does confess man's sinfulness and God's righteousness: "And do not enter into judgment with Your servant, for in Your sight no man living is righteous" (verse 2). David teaches us the value of confession in our approach to God. A good plan for prayer is easily remembered with the word ACTS—Adoration, Confession, Thanksgiving, and Supplication. Notice that confession precedes requests (supplication). David confessed before he asked, and so must we. In what way do you think confession paves the way for asking God for our needs? You might read 1 John 1:9 as you think about your response.

3. Read Psalm 143:1-7 and write your observations about how David talked with God. What did he talk about, and what did he ask of God?

4. Notice that David relies on the faithfulness and righteousness of God for the answers to his prayers. You can rely on God's character when you pray. Meditate on the following verses and underline the words and phrases that are significant to you about who God is and what God promises He will fulfill.

> "In Your righteousness deliver me and rescue me; incline Your ear to me and save me. Be to me a rock of habitation to which I may continually come; You have given commandment to save me, for You are my rock and my fortress" (Psalm 71:2-3).

> "I will sing of the lovingkindness of the LORD forever; to all generations I will make known Your faithfulness with my mouth. For I have said, 'Lovingkindness will be built up forever; in the heavens You will establish Your faithfulness'" (Psalm 89:1-2).

> "Splendid and majestic is His work, and His righteousness endures forever" (Psalm 111:3).

> "This I recall to mind, therefore I have hope. The LORD's lovingkindnesses indeed never cease, for His compassions never fail. They are new every morning; great is Your faithfulness" (Lamentations 3:21-23).

"God is faithful, through whom you were called into fellowship with His Son, Jesus Christ our Lord" (1 Corinthians 1:9).

"Let us hold fast the confession of our hope without wavering, for He who promised is faithful" (Hebrews 10:23).

ADORE GOD IN PRAYER

Paul encourages you in Philippians 4:6-7 to "be anxious for nothing, but in everything by prayer and supplication with thanksgiving let your requests be made known to God. And the peace of God, which surpasses all comprehension, will guard your hearts and your minds in Christ Jesus." Will you take all your anxieties and burdens to your Lord today, letting "your requests be made known to God"? Devote a prayer page in the back of this book to all the requests on your heart. Be sure to date each request so you can track how and when God answers your prayers.

YIELD YOURSELF TO GOD

He who has given us the privilege of prayer never tires of us, even though we never do anything else when we pray than to ask of Him. But He does desire to teach us also to converse with Him in prayer...He desires to share with you the little things of life. That is always the way when two people love each other. They share everything, little things as well as big things, their joys as well as their sorrows. That is what makes love so rich and so joyous. Speak, therefore, with God about your daily experiences. They need not be great or important. Speak with Him about the little things which make up your daily life. Tell God when you are happy. Let Him share your joy. That is what He is waiting to do. Tell God when you are sad, when you are worried, when you do not know what to do, when you are anxious. He is waiting to hear about it because He loves you. This being the case, nothing is inconsequential or unimportant. Everything that concerns you interests Him. God never intended that we should live our Christian life in any other way. Everyday Christianity cannot be practiced unless we incessantly receive into our lives that supply of spiritual power which is necessary in order to preserve within us that spirit which is willing to deny self, to serve others, to endure wrong and to let others have the last word. Furthermore, God desires to be with us in all of our daily struggles. He desires to help us and make even our purely temporal tasks easier. So completely does He give Himself to us. He desires to share everything with us. This is the best part of our whole Christian life. Nothing is so blessed as quiet, unbroken communication with our Lord. The sense of the Lord's nearness, which then fills our souls, is greater than any other peace, joy, inner satisfaction, or security which we have known. Even adversity and sorrow lose their sting when we share everything with our Lord.[2]

ENJOY HIS PRESENCE

What have you learned from David's example that will help you in talking with God?

REST IN HIS LOVE

"I stretch out my hands to You; my soul longs for You, as a parched land" (Psalm 143:6).

FOR TEACHING

Let me hear Your lovingkindness in the morning;
For I trust in You;
Teach me the way in which I should walk;
For to You I lift up my soul.

PSALM 143:8

PREPARE YOUR HEART

One of the best prayers in the Bible was made by the disciples to Jesus, "Lord, teach us to pray" (Luke 11:1). The more you spend time with God in His Word and in prayer, the more you will learn how to pray and what to pray. A person with a willing heart, open to learning from God, is teachable and makes the most progress in the school of prayer. This is one of your greatest prayer requests: "Teach me, Lord." Ask Him to teach you about every aspect of your life—how to live, love, work, and pray. You can even ask Him how to live in the difficult times, for He is the one who indeed knows the way.

You may have heard the story of the man who fell into a deep hole. Several people walked past the man in trouble. One wrote a prayer on a piece of paper and threw it into the hole. Another tried to comfort the man by saying he would pray for him. Finally, one man walked up to the hole and jumped in. The man in trouble looked at the man as though he was crazy and said, "Why did you do that? Now we're both in trouble." The other man looked at him, smiled, and said, "No we're not. I've been in this hole before, and I know the way out."

David knew the secret of the teachable heart in the school of prayer. He often asked the Lord to teach him in his walk with God. Draw near to the Lord today and ask Him to give you a teachable heart so that you might grow and learn all He has to teach you.

READ AND STUDY GOD'S WORD

1. Read Psalm 143:8-12 and write out everything that David wanted to learn from the Lord.

2. Read Psalm 25, also written by David, and write out what you learn about the Lord's instruction. Who does the Lord instruct? And what will He teach us?

3. What is your most significant insight from Psalm 25 about the Lord's instruction in your life?

4. What will be the result of a teachable heart? Read Isaiah 66:2 and write your insights.

ADORE GOD IN PRAYER

What do you desire to learn from the Lord? Will you ask the Lord to teach you?

> Make me know Your ways, O LORD;
> Teach me Your paths.
> Lead me in Your truth and teach me,
> For You are the God of my salvation;
> For You I wait all the day (Psalm 25:4-5).

YIELD YOURSELF TO GOD

A side gorge that sweeps up to the glaciers and snowy pyramids flashing upon you in the opposite direction is the route which you suppose your guide is going to take; and visions of pedestrians perilously scaling icy precipices, or struggling up to the middle through ridges of snow, begin to surround you, as the prospect of your own experience in this day's expedition. So convinced was I that the path *must* go in that direction, that I took the short cut, which I conceived would bring me again into the mule path at a point under the glaciers; but after scaling precipices and getting lost in a wood of firs in the valley, I was glad to rejoin my friend with the guide, and to clamber on in pure ignorance and wonder...

Now what a striking symbol is this of things that sometimes take place in our spiritual pilgrimage. We are often brought to a stand, hedged up and hemmed in by the providence of God so that there seems no way out. A man is sometimes thrown into difficulties in which he sits down beginning to despair, and says to himself, "Well, this time it is all over with me"; like Sterne's starling, or, worse, like Bunyan's man in the cage, he says, "I cannot get out." Then when God has drawn him from all self-confidence and self-resource, a door opens in the wall and he rises up, and walks at liberty, praising God.[3]

CHARLES SPURGEON

ENJOY HIS PRESENCE

When Mary met Jesus in the garden after He rose from the dead, she recognized Him as "Rabboni," which means "Teacher" (John 20:16). The Lord is your Teacher as well, and His Word, the Bible, is a library of 66 books filled with spiritual principles He will use in your life to help you grow. Each day we need to resolve to open His Word and hear what He has to say to us. Here is a good prayer for learning from your Lord: "Deal bountifully with Your servant, that I may live and keep Your word. Open my eyes, that I may behold wonderful things from Your law" (Psalm 119:17-18). May this be your prayer request to your Lord throughout this day. Close your time today with the Lord by writing a prayer in your journal in the back of this book.

REST IN HIS LOVE

"Good and upright is the LORD; therefore He instructs sinners in the way. He leads the humble in justice, and He teaches the humble His way" (Psalm 25:8-9).

FOR GUIDANCE

Teach me to do Your will,
For You are my God;
Let Your good Spirit lead me on level ground.
PSALM 143:10

PREPARE YOUR HEART

Billy Graham shares a powerful answer to a prayer for guidance in his book *Just As I Am*. He was eating lunch at a roadside diner in New Jersey. While eating, he was greeted by a big smiling man who immediately recognized him, "What an answer to prayer! I was just sitting here praying that I might meet Billy Graham, and in you walk! I didn't even know you were on the East Coast." He continued, "I have a great burden on my heart. It's a message that I believe is from the Lord. Billy, you must go on national radio…you're the man God could use to touch America through radio." The man urged him to contact his son-in-law, Fred Dienert, and Walter Bennett, a Christian who was a radio agent. Billy was so busy that he dismissed the entire idea.

A few weeks later while speaking at a conference in Michigan, Billy was approached by Mr. Dienert and Mr. Bennett about broadcasting a national radio program. At the time Billy was president of Northwestern schools, active with Youth for Christ, and addressing the national interest in the evangelistic crusades. He consulted his close advisors who agreed; now was just not the time for a radio program.

Later, in Portland, the two men approached him again. Billy was annoyed by their persistence and sometimes took a back elevator to avoid them. He instructed those on his team to tell the men he was simply not interested in broadcasting. As he came out of the hotel one night, he was approached by the men again. "We want to say good-bye," they said. "We're leaving for Chicago."

Billy laughed and said, "All right, fellows, if before midnight tonight I should get $25,000 for the purpose of a radio broadcast, I'll take that as an answer to prayer and be willing to do a national broadcast." Realizing how outrageous that request was, they laughed along with Billy and headed for the airport. More than 17,000 people attended the meeting. Billy shared the burden of Dienert and Bennett for broadcasting the gospel and the $25,000 condition. The audience laughed along with Billy.

After the meeting, Billy greeted many of those in attendance. Several indicated their desire to help Billy go on national radio and gave him cash, checks, and pledges. Billy was overwhelmed! When they added up the money, the total was $24,000. Billy wept at the generosity and faith of so many. But Billy thought, "How could this be God's answer? It's $1000 short." When his group arrived at their hotel that night, they were greeted by the hotel clerk. "There are two letters here for you, Mr. Graham." They were postmarked two days earlier, from businessmen Billy hardly knew. He opened the letters. Both businessmen said they believed that Billy should go on radio, and they wanted to contribute to that ministry. Each enclosed a $500 check! Billy bowed his head and spoke with God. Overcome with emotion, he turned to go to the elevator—and there stood Dienert and Bennett! They had gone to the airport but felt led by the Lord to go back to the hotel. Billy put his hands on the shoulders of both men and said, "Sign us up for radio for at least thirteen weeks. God has answered prayer. We have the $25,000. We'll take this as a step of faith." Those thirteen weeks of broadcasting became the well-known radio show *The Hour of Decision*.

God has promised to lead each one of us on His path to accomplish His will. And though we are sometimes unsure of the way to go, we can be confident of His leading. Our best prayer is, "Teach me to do Your will, for You are my God; let Your good Spirit lead me on level ground." We want to *know* His will, but even more, we must desire to *do* His will. He gives us the Holy Spirit, the Comforter, to lead us and strengthen us to accomplish God's will (John 14:16; Acts 1:8; Romans 8:14; Colossians 1:11).

Today, ask the Lord to teach you to know and do His will.

READ AND STUDY GOD'S WORD

1. Read Psalm 143:10 and write out the phrase that is most significant to you.

2. The Bible is filled with instruction and promises about God's will and God's leading in your life. Look at the following verses and write out all that you learn about His leading and guidance.

Psalm 16:11

Psalm 23:3

Psalm 31:3

Psalm 48:14

Psalm 73:23-24

Psalm 119:105

Proverbs 3:5-6

Isaiah 58:11

Romans 8:14

James 1:5

3. Summarize in two or three sentences what you have learned about God's leading and guidance.

4. Can you think of a time when God led you in a new direction or answered your prayer for wisdom and guidance?

ADORE GOD IN PRAYER

Good morning, Lord! What are You up to today? Can I be a part of it? Thank You.
Amen.

NORMAN GRUBB

YIELD YOURSELF TO GOD

God wants your prayer life to be filled with petitions and intercessions for others
and for the advance of His kingdom. He wants answers to such prayer to become
your thrilling and frequent experience. One of the great joys of prayer is securing
wonderful answers that seem so long delayed and so humanly impossible. God
wants answers to your prayers to be frequent and blessed. He wants you to prove
repeatedly the mighty power of prayer in your own experience. He wants you to
become not only a prayer veteran but also a constant victor in situations where
the answers bring great glory to God and great consternation and defeat to Satan.
He wants you to experience frequently His prayer-answering power, His intensely
personal concern and love for you, and the tremendously varied means available to
His wisdom. God is never perplexed or surprised, and never ultimately defeated.
He desires you, through prayer, to share in bringing His will to pass on earth.[4]

WESLEY L. DUEWEL

ENJOY HIS PRESENCE

When you ask the Lord for guidance, you can rest on His promise: "The steps of a man are
established by the LORD, and He delights in his way. When He falls, he will not be hurled head-
long, because the LORD is the One who holds his hand" (Psalm 37:23-24). How do you need
God's guidance today? Write a prayer to the Lord in your journal, expressing all that is on your
heart.

REST IN HIS LOVE

"And the LORD will continually guide you, and satisfy your desire in scorched places, and give
strength to your bones; and you will be like a watered garden, and like a spring of water whose
waters do not fail" (Isaiah 58:11).

FOR PERSONAL REVIVAL

For the sake of Your name, O LORD, revive me.
In Your righteousness bring my soul out of trouble.
PSALM 143:11

PREPARE YOUR HEART

Sometimes your heart and soul will experience trouble. Whether you are enduring a profound loss, a nagging illness, or a desolate wilderness, you need a special answer from God. You need what only He can give—personal spiritual revival. Personal revival is a quickening of the heart and soul, restoring you to the plans and purposes of God. You need personal revival when you are confronted with sin, suffering, or the need for spiritual growth. The psalmists are champions at expressing their need for revival. Repeatedly you will discover their prayer—Revive me—and their confident declarations of trust—You will revive me. Draw near to God today and pray, *Revive me, O Lord.*

READ AND STUDY GOD'S WORD

1. David's heart was dry and thirsty. He said, "I stretch out my hands to You; my soul longs for You, as a parched land" (Psalm 143:6). Then he prays for revival. Read again our verse for today and write out your own paraphrase.

2. Read the following verses in the psalms and write what you learn about revival:

Psalm 71:20

Psalm 80:18

Psalm 119:25,37,50,107

Psalm 138:7

3. Write out your most significant insight about personal revival.

ADORE GOD IN PRAYER

Pray the prayer of David today: "For the sake of Your name, O LORD, revive me. In Your righteousness bring my soul out of trouble."

YIELD YOURSELF TO GOD

> We who believe the promise of God should rejoice in the prospect of divine revivals in our souls, and as we experience them our holy joy should overflow. Are we thirsting? Let us not murmur, but sing…let us ask that the Scripture we have read, and our devotional exercises, may not be an empty formality, but a channel of grace to our souls. O that God the Holy Spirit would work in us with all his mighty power, filling us with all the fullness of God.[5]
>
> CHARLES SPURGEON

ENJOY HIS PRESENCE

In what ways do you need revival today? Are there any areas of your life that seem like a "parched land" (Psalm 143:6)? Write your thoughts in your journal and then close by writing a prayer to the Lord.

REST IN HIS LOVE

"Though I walk in the midst of trouble, you will revive me; you will stretch forth Your hand against the wrath of my enemies, and Your right hand will save me" (Psalm 138:7).

FOR DELIVERANCE

And in Your lovingkindness, cut off my enemies
And destroy all those who afflict my soul,
For I am Your servant.
PSALM 143:12

PREPARE YOUR HEART

Sometimes you will face trials that require prevailing prayer. This kind of prayer requires patience and waiting on God, believing He is at work behind the scenes accomplishing deliverance on your behalf. In such situations, you will learn to "pray through" to the other side of your difficulty.

Charles Alexander, successor to Ira B. Sankey as songleader for D.L. Moody, was an evangelist, worship leader, and compiler of several volumes of hymns. He accompanied R.A. Torrey on an evangelistic crusade and led more than 4000 people in worship. He and his wife organized the Pocket Testament League, challenging 2,000,000 people to carry a Bible with them and read a chapter a day. Five weeks before his death in 1920 he inaugurated a Bible revival campaign with other pastors in the Methodist and Presbyterian churches.

One day, during a particularly difficult challenge, Alexander was standing at a bank counter in Liverpool, waiting for a clerk to come and help him. He picked up a pen and began to print on some scratch paper two words that had been on his heart: *pray through.* He kept printing those words again and again, filling every line on the paper. Finally the clerk came, and Alexander transacted his business at the bank and left, leaving the paper behind. A businessman, discouraged from trouble in his company, came to the bank soon after Alexander left. He began to transact business with the same clerk, and the piece of scratch paper caught his eye. He read the words, *pray through.* He exclaimed, "That is the exact message I need! I will pray through. I have tried in my own strength to worry through, and have merely mentioned my troubles to God; now I am going to pray the situation through until I get light."[6]

Draw near to God and ask Him to give you endurance and patience to pray until you experience His answer, His deliverance.

Read and Study God's Word

1. David ends his prayer in Psalm 143 with a cry to God for deliverance from his enemies. He pleads deliverance on the grounds that he is God's servant. David knew something that you can also know: When God hears your cries, He delivers. In fact, God is a God of deliverances (Psalm 68:20). Spend time meditating on each of these verses and write what you learn about deliverance:

Psalm 18:2

Psalm 32:7

Psalm 40:17

Psalm 68:20

Psalm 108:12

Psalm 144:2

2. Summarize what you learned about God's deliverance.

ADORE GOD IN PRAYER

Long is the way, and very steep the slope,
Strengthen me once again, O God of Hope.
Far, very far, the summit doth appear;
But Thou art near my God, but Thou art near.
And Thou wilt give me with my daily food,
Powers of endurance, courage, fortitude.
Thy way is perfect; only let that way
Be clear before my feet from day to day.
Thou art my Portion, saith my soul to Thee,
O what a Portion is my God to me.[7]

AMY CARMICHAEL

YIELD YOURSELF TO GOD

Child of God, today there are obstacles in your life which seem to doom you to utter failure of God's highest purpose for you. You have planned, worried, toiled and failed. Despair is beginning to settle down upon you, and hope is fading away from your life, for all your doing has been thwarted. Try now the asking which brings His doing. Begin to live the prayer life. Ask, ask, ask, and then out of all the failure of your doing look unto Him who says, "If you ask, I will do." Pray—and He will soften hearts which all your doing could never touch; pray—and He will heal that cruel estrangement which is slowly crushing you; pray—and He will meet your needs, both temporal and spiritual; pray—and He will weave all the tangled threads of your life which seem beyond hope of disentanglement into the single golden strand of His great purpose for you; pray—and unto your life, fresh from the failure and disappointment of your doing, He will bring miracles of His doing which will some glad day fill your lips with songs of praise; pray—and He will work changes unthought of, and bring about providences undreamed of; pray—and He will overturn and overturn, until darkness changes to light, bondage to liberty, bridgeless chasms to safe highways, granite walls to webs of gossamer, because a miracle working God has fulfilled His promise, "If ye ask, I will do."[8]

JAMES MCCONKEY

ENJOY HIS PRESENCE

> Don't stop praying, but have more trust;
> Don't stop praying! For pray we must;
> Faith will banish a mount of care;
> Don't stop praying! God answers prayer.[9]

CHARLES ALEXANDER

REST IN HIS LOVE

"God is to us a God of deliverances; and to God the Lord belong escapes from death" (Psalm 68:20).

DEVOTIONAL READING BY CHARLES SPURGEON

Childlike confidence makes us pray as none else can. It causes a man to pray for great things that he would never have asked for if he had not learned this confidence. It also causes him to pray for little things that many people are afraid to ask for, because they have not yet felt toward God the confidence of children. I have often felt that it requires more confidence in God to pray to Him about a little thing than about great things. We imagine that our great things are somehow worthy of God's attention, though in truth they are little enough to Him. And then we think that our little things must be so insignificant that it is an insult to bring them before Him. We need to realize that what is very important to a child may be very small to his parent, and yet the parent measures the thing not from his own point of view but from the child's. You heard your little boy the other day crying bitterly. The cause of the pain was a splinter in his finger. While you did not call in three surgeons to extract it, the splinter was a great thing to that little sufferer. Standing there with eyes all wet through tears of anguish, it never occurred to that boy that his pain was too small a thing for you to care about. What were mothers and fathers made for but to look after the small concerns of little children? And God our Father is a good father who pities us as fathers pity their children. He counts the stars and calls them all by name, yet He heals the broken in heart and binds up their wounds.[10]

Take some time now to write about all that you have learned this week. What has been most significant to you? Write a prayer to the Lord, expressing all that is on your heart.

PRAYER WHEN YOU ARE IN TROUBLE

PSALM 77

It is a glorious thing to have a big trouble, a great Atlantic billow, that takes you off your feet and sweeps you right out to sea, and lets you sink down into the depths, into old ocean's lowest caverns, till you get to the foundation of the mountains, and there see God, and then come up again to tell what a great God He is, and how graciously He delivers His people.

SPRINGS IN THE VALLEY

WHERE DO YOU RUN?

In the day of my trouble I sought the Lord;
In the night my hand was stretched out without weariness;
My soul refused to be comforted.
PSALM 77:2

PREPARE YOUR HEART

Jim Cymbala's daughter, Chrissy, in rebellion, left the safety of their home and disappeared to roam the streets of New York City. As a father who so greatly loved his daughter, Jim was beside himself with agonizing concern and brokenheartedness over her rebellion. One Tuesday night, when he felt overwhelmed, a young woman passed a note to Jim, indicating her desire to pray for Chrissy. He hesitated, unsure whether such a personal request should be presented to the church that evening. And yet something in the note seemed to ring true for him.

He picked up the microphone and said, "Although I haven't talked much about it...my daughter is very far from God these days. She thinks up is down, and down is up; dark is light, and light is dark. But I know God can break through to her, and so I'm going to ask Pastor Boekstaaf to lead us in praying for Chrissy. Let's all join hands across the sanctuary." In describing the experience, Jim Cymbala says the sanctuary became a labor room of prayer—a sense of determination came over everyone present as they poured their hearts out to the Lord for a change of heart in Chrissy.

When Jim returned home that night, he told his wife, Carol, "It's over."

"What's over?"

"It's over with Chrissy. You would have had to be in the prayer meeting tonight. I tell you, if there's a God in heaven, this whole nightmare is finally over." Then he described what had happened.

A few nights later, Chrissy showed up on the doorstep and collapsed into her father's arms. "Daddy, Daddy I've sinned against God. I've sinned against you and mother. And I've sinned against myself. Please forgive me." As she was in the middle of sobbing, she pulled back and said, "Daddy, who was praying for me? On Tuesday night, who was praying for me?" Tuesday night was when she had her great heart turnaround. Her heart was completely changed, she enrolled in Bible school, directed choirs, and later became a pastor's wife and mother to three wonderful children.[1]

Where do you run when you are in trouble? Ask the Lord today to speak to your heart and show you how to run to Him and cry out in prayer.

READ AND STUDY GOD'S WORD

1. This week you are going to live in Psalm 77, written by Asaph, the worship leader appointed by David (1 Chronicles 16:5; 2 Chronicles 29:30). Asaph is the author of a number of psalms in the Bible (Psalms 50; 73–83). Psalm 77 is written for fellow sufferers and provides us with secrets to help us pray and focus on the Lord in our difficulties. Read Psalm 77 and write out your most significant insight.

2. Read Psalm 77:1-10 and write out everything you learn about Asaph's trouble and his suffering.

3. What do you learn about prayer from Asaph's words in Psalm 77:1-2?

4. The psalmists encourage you to cry out to God in your trouble. Read the following verses and write what you learn about prayer and God's help in a time of trouble:

Psalm 9:9-10

Psalm 25:17-18

Psalm 27:5

Psalm 31:7-8

Psalm 34:6,17

Psalm 50:15

Psalm 55:17

ADORE GOD IN PRAYER

Did you notice Asaph's words "I am so troubled that I cannot speak"? Those are the days to lay your burdens out before the Lord. Take your worries, cares, fears, heartbreaks, and shattered dreams and place them in the able hands of the Lord. Then go out into the day in His strength and watch to see what He will do. Talk with Him now about all that is on your heart.

YIELD YOURSELF TO GOD

A train of sorrows moves along this page. Relief is found in drawing near to God, and meditating on His wondrous works. We may have like sufferings. May we find like rescue! Before the Psalmist delineates his grievous state, he openly avows the actions of his soul, and the remedy obtained. His voice was uplifted in earnest and repeated cries to God. He sowed good seed, and reaped success. Happy would be our case, if we converted sufferings into prayers, and made them gates of heaven. Let this be our resolve. It will turn darkness into light.[2]

HENRY LAW

ENJOY HIS PRESENCE

Have you learned the secret of converting sufferings into prayers? Those who are passionate in prayer have learned this secret. Clearly Asaph had resolved to pray in the midst of his trouble because he said, "My voice rises to God, and I will cry aloud." He was confident of God's responsiveness in his trouble, for he said, "My voice rises to God, and He *will* hear me." Think about your own resolve to pray. Join with the psalmist and say, "He will hear my voice" (Psalm 55:17). Always pray first, not last. Your knowledge of God and confidence in His response will fuel your prayers even if you are, like Asaph, so troubled you cannot speak. What is the most important truth you've learned today, offering you hope in a time of trouble?

REST IN HIS LOVE

"Call upon Me in the day of trouble; I shall rescue you, and you will honor Me" (Psalm 50:15).

WILL YOU REMEMBER?

I will remember my song in the night;
I will meditate with my heart,
And my spirit ponders.
PSALM 77:6

PREPARE YOUR HEART

What do you think about when you are experiencing a difficulty in life? Where is your focus and attention? Asaph uses a repeated word in Psalm 77, offering a secret that will encourage your own consistency in prayer. The word *remember* is used four times. The Hebrew word translated "remember" is *zakar* and means to pay special attention to something with great care and concern. Asaph remembered God—who He is, what He does, and what He says. When you remember God, your focus on Him will help you continue to run the race God has set before you, even in the midst of a great loss or a painful trial. Your remembrance of God does not diminish the nature of your difficulty, but it strengthens you with comfort and peace. Begin your quiet time today with Psalm 34. Meditate on these words of David written in a time of trouble. Write out your favorite promise from this psalm.

READ AND STUDY GOD'S WORD

1. Read Psalm 77:1-11 and write out everything you learn about Asaph's habit of remembering. What, when, and how did he remember?

2. Taking time to remember God is a practice that will greatly encourage your heart and soul. Read the following verses and write out what you learn about setting aside some time with your Lord in solitude so you can remember:

Psalm 46:10

Isaiah 30:15

Mark 6:30-32

James 4:8

3. Notice that Asaph remembered his "song in the night." The Lord will give you a song even in the night. Your song will consist of truths from His Word that have encouraged your heart and that become a prayer you sing to Him. Read the following verses and underline the words and phrases most significant to you about the song from the Lord:

"The LORD is my strength and my shield; my heart trusts in Him, and I am helped; therefore my heart exults, and with my song I shall thank Him" (Psalm 28:7).

"You are my hiding place; You preserve me from trouble; You surround me with songs of deliverance" (Psalm 32:7).

"Sing to Him a new song; play skillfully with a shout of joy" (Psalm 33:3).

"He put a new song in my mouth, a song of praise to our God; many will see and fear and will trust in the LORD" (Psalm 40:3).

"The LORD will command His lovingkindness in the daytime; and His song will be with me in the night, a prayer to the God of my life" (Psalm 42:8).

"The LORD is my strength and song, And He has become my salvation" (Psalm 118:14).

"Your statutes are my songs in the house of my pilgrimage. O LORD, I remember Your name in the night, and keep your law. This has become mine, that I observe Your precepts" (Psalm 119:54-56).

ADORE GOD IN PRAYER

Talk with God today about all that is on your heart. Begin by praying through the verses you remembered in Read and Study God's Word.

YIELD YOURSELF TO GOD

Charles Haddon Spurgeon is one who knew trials of affliction and sorrow. He wrote his commentaries on the Psalms, *The Treasury of David,* over a period of 20 years (1865–1885). During those years, the man known by many as the "prince of preachers" suffered neuralgia, gout, debilitating headaches, and frightening bouts of depression. He writes about his songs in the night:

> No doubt Paul and Silas remembered their song in the night, when imprisoned at Philippi; and it afforded them encouragement under subsequent trials. And cannot many of you, my brethren, in like manner, remember the supports and consolations you have enjoyed in former difficulties, and how the Lord turned the shadow of death into morning? And ought you not to trust to him that hath delivered, that he will yet deliver? He that hath delivered in six troubles will not forsake you in seven. The "clouds may return after the rain"; but not a drop can fall without the leave of him, who rides on the heavens for your help, and in his excellency on the sky. Did you not forbode at first a very different termination of the former troubles and did not the Lord disappoint your fears, and put a new song into your mouth; and will you not now begin to trust him, and triumph in him? Surely you have found that the Lord can clear the darkest skies.[3]

ENJOY HIS PRESENCE

The night is sometimes the most difficult time when a person is in trouble. The mind is more susceptible to fear and worries. Notice that Asaph remembered his song *in the night,* meditated with his heart, and pondered with his spirit. The Word of God will give you words for your song and truths for your meditation. As you think about what you've learned from God's Word today, what is your song to the Lord? Close your quiet time by writing your song to Him in your journal.

REST IN HIS LOVE

"For thus the Lord GOD, the Holy One of Israel, has said, 'In repentance and rest you will be saved, in quietness and trust is your strength'" (Isaiah 30:15).

WHAT HAS GOD PROMISED?

Has His lovingkindness ceased forever?
Has His promise come to an end forever?
PSALM 77:8

PREPARE YOUR HEART

When you are in a time of trouble, you may feel insecure and shaken, with no solid ground beneath your feet. One woman shared that in those times, she reminds herself of the solid foundation of God's Word by literally standing on her Bible. The Bible is filled with promises from God, custom-designed for your particular need. For example, when you feel as though the floodwaters of your life are overwhelming you, take heart in the promise of Isaiah 43:2: "When you pass through the waters, I will be with you; and through the rivers, they will not overflow you." When your heart is broken, you can know that "the LORD is near to the brokenhearted and saves those who are crushed in spirit" (Psalm 34:18). When chaos seems to rule your day, you can take comfort in the fact that your times are in God's hand (Psalm 31:15). Learn to stand firmly on the promises of your God.

Begin your quiet time today by meditating on the words of the hymn "Standing on the Promises":

> Standing on the promises of Christ my King!
> Through eternal ages let His praises ring.
> "Glory in the highest!" I will shout and sing,
> Standing on the promises of God.

> Standing on the promises that cannot fail,
> When the howling storms of doubt and fear assail.
> By the living Word of God I shall prevail,
> Standing on the promises of God.

Standing on the promises I now can see
Perfect, present cleansing in the blood for me;
Standing in the liberty where Christ makes free,
Standing on the promises of God.

Standing on the promises of Christ, the Lord,
Bound to Him eternally by love's strong cord,
Overcoming daily with the Spirit's sword,
Standing on the promises of God.

Standing on the promises I cannot fall,
List'ning every moment to the Spirit's call,
Resting in my Savior as my All in All,
Standing on the promises of God.

Standing, standing, Standing on the promises of God my Savior;
Standing, standing, I'm standing on the promises of God.

R. KELSO CARTER

READ AND STUDY GOD'S WORD

1. When you read the psalms, you discover that the psalmists had great feet of clay and struggled with suffering just as we do. Alan Redpath, former pastor of Moody Church in Chicago and author of a book on the life of David, makes this observation:

> The Bible never flatters its heroes. It tells us the truth about each one of them in order that against the background of human breakdown and failure we may magnify the grace of God and recognize that it is the delight of the Spirit of God to work upon the platform of human impossibilities. As we consider the record of Bible characters, how often we find ourselves looking into a mirror. We are humiliated by the reminder of how many times we have failed. Great has been our stubbornness but greater still has been His faithfulness.[4]

Redpath's words are an encouragement to us in our own failures of faith and trust in God. Asaph was a faithful servant of God who struggled with doubt and discouragement. In Psalm 73, Asaph speaks candidly of his envy of the arrogant, who never seemed to have any problems. He then reveals what he discovered when he finally drew near to God (Psalm 73:17). In Psalm 77,

Asaph shares a series of six rhetorical questions, revealing his own wrestling with his feelings and what he knows to be true in God's Word. Read Psalm 77:7-9 and write out the focus of each of Asaph's questions.

2. Asaph knew what was true in God's Word. But his circumstances seemed to contradict what God had said. So Asaph was faced with a choice. Would he hold to God's Word, resulting in hope, or would he focus on his circumstances and fall into despair? Asaph chose wisely and turned his thoughts to remember the character and works of God. God's promises throughout Scripture reveal who God is, what God does, and what He says. In fact, you can discover truths about God in every passage of the Bible. The promises of God have been likened to checks drawn on an unlimited account backed by the very Creator of the heaven and earth Himself. The question is, will you transact business and write a check on the promises of God? Will you attach your name to each promise and take it to God and wait patiently for Him to fulfill His promises in His time and according to His purposes? Read the following verses and write out what you learn about the great value of God's Word in your life:

Matthew 7:24-27

Romans 15:4

2 Peter 1:2-4

3. When you are resting on God's Word and standing on His promises, nothing can shake you. You are steadfast and secure on unshakeable ground. You can sing with the psalmist, "My heart is steadfast, O God; my heart is steadfast; I will sing, yes, I will sing praises!" (Psalm 57:7). You will discover your trust in God becomes stronger as you focus on the promises of God. Read Jeremiah 17:5-8 and write what you learn about the steadfastness of a person who trusts in God.

ADORE GOD IN PRAYER

Talk with God today about your need to focus on His promises. Then, pray through the hymn "Standing on the Promises," directing the words to your Lord as a resolve and commitment to focus on His promises.

YIELD YOURSELF TO GOD

We want to be more business like and use common sense with God in pleading promises. If you were to go to one of the banks, and see a man go in and out and lay a piece of paper on the table, and take it up again and nothing more—if he did that several times a day, I think there would soon be orders to keep the man out. Those men who come to the bank in earnest present their checks, they wait until they receive their gold, and then they go; but not without having transacted real business. They do not put the paper down, speak about the excellent signature, and discuss the excellent document; but they want their money for it, and they are not content without it. These are the people who are always welcome at the bank, and not triflers. Alas, a great many people play at praying. They do not expect God to give them an answer, and thus they are mere triflers. Our heavenly Father would have us do real business with Him in our praying.[5]

CHARLES SPURGEON

ENJOY HIS PRESENCE

What is the most important truth you have learned today? How do you need God's promises? How will the promises of God help your prayers? What is your favorite promise that will encourage you to stand strong?

REST IN HIS LOVE

"And because of his glory and excellence, he has given us great and precious promises. These are the promises that enable you to share his divine nature and escape the world's corruption caused by human desires" (2 Peter 1:4 NLT).

WHO IS YOUR GOD?

Your way, O God, is holy;
What god is great like our God?
PSALM 77:13

PREPARE YOUR HEART

Asaph turned his thoughts to the character and works of God, moving from doubt and discouragement to hope and faith. The result was a great hope. Paul says, "For whatever was written in earlier times was written for our instruction, so that through perseverance and encouragement of the Scriptures we might have hope" (Romans 15:4). Paul's words reveal the importance of opening the pages of God's Word in a time of trouble. What value will you gain by reading and studying your Bible? You will be encouraged. And ultimately you will be a person of HOPE—Holding On with Patient Expectation. Today, ask God to fill your heart with encouragement and hope.

READ AND STUDY GOD'S WORD

1. Asaph moved from his questions of doubt to contemplations of God. Notice as you read his words how his observations *about* God quickly moved to conversation *with* God. Here you see how Asaph is taken from a focus on his circumstances to a faith in God and God's abiding presence in his life. Whenever you are in God's Word, you will be moved to prayer. Read Psalm 77:11-20 and write out everything you learn about God.

2. What truth about God encourages you the most today and why?

ADORE GOD IN PRAYER

May I love you, my God and Father, with a holy, absorbing, and increasing love, not for what you give, but for who you are.[6]

F.B. MEYER

YIELD YOURSELF TO GOD

When you focus on the character of God, you become more aware of His presence and power, especially as you are moved to talk with Him in prayer. Meditate on these words by Hannah Whitall Smith about the secret of His presence:

The "secret of His presence" is a more secure refuge than a thousand Gibraltars. I do not mean that no trials will come. They may come in abundance, but they cannot penetrate into the sanctuary of the soul, and we may dwell in perfect peace even in the midst of life's fiercest storms…

We must make up our minds to move into our dwelling place in God and to take there with us all our possessions, above all, those we love. We must hide ourselves in Him away from ourselves, away from all others, and we must lose sight of everything that is outside of Him except as we see it through His eyes. God's eyes are the windows of God's house, and the only windows there are; and seen through His eyes, all things will put on a new aspect. We shall see our trials as blessings, and our enemies as disguised friends. We shall be calm and at rest in the face of all the frets and worries of life, untouched by any of them. "And my people shall dwell in a peaceable habitation, and in sure dwellings, and in quiet resting places" (Isaiah 32:18 KJV).[7]

ENJOY HIS PRESENCE

Asaph found such encouragement in his contemplation of God. And so will you. Henry Law describes how your focus on God will change your entire perspective:

Reviving faith returns to God, and drooping doubts are cast aside. It flies on renovated wings to contemplate God's wonder-working hand. It enters the precious treasury full of past records. Here it finds renewal of assurance. Happy meditation traverses the path impressed by heavenly footsteps.[8]

Oh, that you may know that "happy meditation" in your life today.

REST IN HIS LOVE

"You are the God who works wonders; You have made known Your strength among the peoples" (Psalm 77:14).

WHAT HAS GOD DONE?

You led Your people like a flock.
PSALM 77:20

PREPARE YOUR HEART

Sometimes the storms of life may rage with such ferocity you may feel like giving up. And yet, when you read the Bible, you discover God encourages you to stand strong. Again and again, you will read exhortations like these: "Be strong in the Lord and in the strength of His might" (Ephesians 6:10), and "Be steadfast, immovable, always abounding in the work of the Lord, knowing that your toil is not in vain in the Lord" (1 Corinthians 15:58). How can you keep going when everything seems to drive you toward despair? Focus on what God has done. Remember His ways. What you've seen God do in the past will encourage you in the present. Remembering the work of God strengthens your belief in the word of God. What He has done for those saints in the Bible, He can do for you even now. As you draw near to God today, pray these words written by Peter Marshall: "Wilt Thou give to us that faith that we can deposit in the bank of Thy love, so that we may receive the dividends and interest that Thou art so willing to give us. We ask it all in the lovely name of Jesus Christ our Saviour. Amen."[9]

READ AND STUDY GOD'S WORD

1. Asaph developed the good habit of remembering God—His character and works. Read Psalm 77:11-20 and write out the specific works of God that encouraged you the most today.

2. Knowing that the Lord was his Redeemer and that He had redeemed His people helped Asaph focus on the power of God (Psalm 77:15). Knowing the Lord was his Shepherd and had led His people encouraged Asaph to believe God for personal guidance (Psalm 77:20). Read the following verses and record your insights related to the works of God. Ask the question as you read, what does God do?

Psalm 23

Psalm 103:2-6

Isaiah 40:11,28-31

Ephesians 3:20-21

3. How does focusing on what God does help you in your own challenges and troubles?

ADORE GOD IN PRAYER

Blessed be Thy Name, Thou ever-living God…Thou abidest the same, and of Thy years there is no end. We come to Thee. Thou art this day as strong to deliver as in our fathers' time; as true to Thy promise, and as mighty to perform Thy Covenant as when Thou spakest unto Abraham at Mamre, or didst work mightily in the field of Zoan for the Children of Israel. Thou, O God, art for ever strong and mighty.[10]

CHARLES SPURGEON

YIELD YOURSELF TO GOD

Believe God's Word and power more than you believe your own feelings and experiences…Do not remain in the haven of distrust, or sleeping on your shadows in inactive repose, or suffering your frames and feelings to pitch and toss on one another like vessels idly moored in a harbor. The religious life is not a brooding over emotions, grazing the keel of faith in the shallows, of dragging the anchor of hope through the oozy tide of mud as if afraid of encountering the healthy breeze. Away! With your canvas spread to the gale, trusting in Him, who rules the raging of the waters. The safety of the tinted bird is to be on the wing. If its haunt be near the ground—if it fly low—it exposes itself to the fowler's net or snare. If we remain groveling on the low ground of feeling and emotion, we shall find ourselves entangled in a thousand meshes of doubt and despondency, temptation and unbelief...Hope thou in God.[11]

Often you cannot get at a difficulty so as to deal with it aright and find your way to a happy result. You pray, but have not the liberty in prayer which you desire. A definite promise is what you want. You try one and another of the inspired words, but they do not fit. You try again, and in due season a promise presents itself which seems to have been made for the occasion; it fits exactly as a well-made key fits the lock for which it was prepared. Having found the identical word of the living God you hasten to plead it at the throne of grace, saying "O Lord, Thou hast promised this good thing unto Thy servant; be pleased to grant it!" The matter is ended: sorrow is turned to joy; prayer is heard.[12]

CHARLES SPURGEON

ENJOY HIS PRESENCE

There will be much about our own lives that may never be clear or understandable. However, there is even more that we can know about our God and rely on when our world is seemingly turned upside down. His promises will keep you sure and steadfast and will lead you to believing prayer. As Henry Law says, "it is our wisdom to trust, when we have no skill to trace...Faith learns the happy lesson, that though God's dealings are inscrutable, no impossibilities can impede Him. The good Shepherd will be a faithful guardian of His flock."[13] Close your time with the Lord today by thanking Him for how He is working in your life.

Faith, mighty faith, the promise sees
And looks to God alone,
Laughs at impossibilities,
And cries, "It shall be done."[14]

Rest in His Love

"Do you not know? Have you not heard? The Everlasting God, the Lord, the Creator of the ends of the earth does not become weary or tired. His understanding is inscrutable. He gives strength to the weary, and to Him who lacks might He increases power" (Isaiah 40:28-29).

DEVOTIONAL READING
BY JOHN HENRY JOWETT

The spirit grows faint and timid when we have no communion with the breath of God. But when we face our perils in communion with the Lord, our timidities are transformed, our uncertainties vanish, and our slipping feet are steadied by being shod with "the preparation of the gospel of peace." Deeper communion with God is the great secret of spiritual maturity. Our preparation for meeting trying and exacting circumstances is often very ill-arranged. We do this, and that, and the other; we fuss around in twenty ways, and our life remains "a haunt of fears." We meet our days with a divided life, and our heart is not fixed in a healthy serenity. We have not the sovereign command which belongs to peace. If only we would put on strength and confidence like a robe... *Take from our lives the strain and stress!* Yes, but who can do that but God? He can do it, and by His grace it is done. In His strengthening, restoring fellowship, we can face all our hostile circumstances with "ordered lives," lives which confess the beauty of God's peace.[15]

Take some time now to write about all that you have learned this week. What has been most significant to you? Close by writing a prayer to the Lord.

PRAYER WHEN YOU ARE THIRSTY

Beloved, God has for us these springs, and we need them every day. Let us drink of the living waters. Nay, let us receive them into our very hearts, so that we shall carry the fountain with us wherever we go.

A.B. Simpson

WHEN YOU ARE IN THE WILDERNESS

O God, You are my God; I shall seek You earnestly;
My soul thirsts for You, my flesh yearns for You,
In a dry and weary land where there is no water.

PSALM 63:1

PREPARE YOUR HEART

In the far-off plains of a Laplander village, a hundred miles from the Polar Sea, at a certain season, a young reindeer will raise his muzzle to the north wind and stare off into the distance for just a moment. He grows restless. The next day a dozen or more of the reindeer herd also look up from their grazing in the moss of the land. Then the Laplanders nod to one another and prepare for their journey. At times, the whole herd of reindeer will stand and gaze, breathing hard through their wide nostrils and stomping the soft ground. They become unruly, making it more and more difficult to harness them into the sleds. The Laplanders watch the reindeer more and more closely, knowing their journey is about to begin.

At last, in the northern twilight, the herd begins to move. Their heads turn in the direction of the Polar Sea. They move slowly at first and then break into a light trot. When they begin to move, the Laplanders pack up their belongings. The great herd moves from a trot to a gallop and then to an even faster pace until the thunder of their movement is gone. They are on their way to drink of the Polar Sea. The Laplanders follow after them, dragging their laden sledges in the tracks left by the thousands of reindeer. The herd resolutely races onward toward their destination, longing only to drink of the water ahead of them. When the Laplanders finally reach the shore, the reindeer are once more quietly grazing, having found the water they have so long desired.

In your pilgrimage with the Lord, you are going to be led into wilderness places. Paul went away to the desert of Arabia for at least three years when he first became a Christian (Galatians 1:17). David was forced to flee to the wilderness by the rebellion of his son Absalom (2 Samuel 15:23). The people of Israel wandered in the wilderness (Exodus 16:35), and Moses pastured the flock of his father-in-law Jethro in the wilderness near Mt. Horeb (Exodus 3:1).

In the wilderness you will experience a thirst, an intense longing for God. Such thirst can only be satisfied by the Lord. The wilderness may seem to be a difficult, desperate time, but it also can be a very precious, intimate time with the Lord. In fact, the wilderness can be the place of deep communion, where you learn how to talk with your Lord. Your passion in prayer will grow when you are in the wilderness. The Lord said in Hosea 2:14, "Therefore, behold, I will allure her, will bring her into the wilderness, and speak comfort to her" (NKJV). And so, dear friend, embrace your wilderness time as your opportunity to draw near to God in a new and deeper way.

READ AND STUDY GOD'S WORD

1. This week we will be living in Psalm 63, which was written by David when he was a king and in danger from his son Absalom (2 Samuel 15–19). Read Psalm 63:1-11 and write the verse that is most significant to you today.

2. Read Psalm 63:1 and describe David's experience.

3. David is clearly in the wilderness experience—a time of intense spiritual thirst and deep suffering. With no earthly reason to smile, David turns his complete attention to the Lord. Oh, what value there is in the desert experience. Read the following verses and record what you learn about the wilderness (or desert) and what God does for you there:

Exodus 16:1-4

Deuteronomy 8:2-3

Psalm 78:15-19

Psalm 136:16

Isaiah 35:7-9

Isaiah 41:17-20

Isaiah 58:11

Hosea 2:14

ADORE GOD IN PRAYER

O God, I have tasted Thy goodness, and it has both satisfied me and made me thirsty for more. I am painfully conscious of my need of further grace. I am ashamed of my lack of desire. O God, the Triune God, I want to want Thee; I long to be filled with longing; I thirst to be made more thirsty still. Show me Thy glory, I pray Thee, so that I may know Thee indeed. Begin in mercy a new work of love within me. Say to my soul, "Rise up, my love, my fair one, and come away." Then give me grace to rise and follow Thee up from this misty lowland where I have wandered so long. In Jesus' name. Amen.[1]

A.W. TOZER

YIELD YOURSELF TO GOD

Life is not easy for any of us, if we regard external conditions only; but directly we learn the divine secret, rivers flow from bare heights, fountains arise in sterile valleys, and the desert blooms like the forest glade. To the ordinary eye there might appear no outward change in the forbidding circumstance; but faith's eye always beholds a paradise of beauty where other eyes see only straitened circumstances and a trying lot.[2]

F.B. MEYER

God shines on thee to make thee fit for life's desert-places—for its Gethsemanes, for its Calvaries. He lifts thee up that He may give thee strength to go farther down; He illuminates thee that He may send thee into the night, that He may make thee a help to the helpless.[3]

The desert, or wilderness, appears in Scripture not just as a place where certain things happened, but as a symbol of isolation in some form—isolation, however, into which God Himself leads us for purposes of discipline and discovery within His love-relation to us. In the desert God will discipline us for the maturing of our faith and character as disciples, and we accept the discipline because we know the spiritual advance is what it will lead to. In the desert, too, God will uncover, and show us, what we are made of spiritually, for it is a place of testing; we shall learn more than we previously knew about our present shortcomings (lovelessness, thoughtlessness, instability, indiscipline, self-absorption, malice, pride, unbelief, disordered desires, and, as the travel brochures say, much, much more); also through God's revelatory action, we shall learn, or relearn, much about him that calls for trust and love and praise (the greatness of His grace, His all-sufficiency, His wisdom and beauty, His faithfulness, His purpose and priorities, and so forth). The desert experience may thus have great significance in our personal pilgrimage.[4]

J. I. PACKER

ENJOY HIS PRESENCE

Take comfort, dear friend, if you should find yourself in the wilderness place. God is in the wilderness places of seeming waste as well as the glorious heights of the mountains. He will meet you in the wilderness and commune with you there. Draw near to Him, and He will draw near to you (James 4:8).

REST IN HIS LOVE

"I will open rivers on the bare heights and springs in the midst of the valleys; I will make the wilderness a pool of water and the dry land fountains of water" (Isaiah 41:18).

PRAISE HIM IN THE WILDERNESS

Because Your lovingkindness is better than life,
My lips will praise You.
PSALM 63:3

PREPARE YOUR HEART

You will discover some of the most beautiful flowers blooming in the wilderness. When you least expect it, you will receive a new experience of God's love, and you will be moved to praise. Your ability to see is refined in the wilderness, for your earthly distractions have most likely been diminished or altogether taken away. Your focus will move from earth to heaven. In the dry and weary land, David experienced God's lovingkindness. The Hebrew word translated "loving-kindness" is *hesed* and refers to God's unchangeable, steady, covenant love. Nothing on earth compares with such love. Nothing satisfies the heart like God's love. And nothing can take away God's love from you. Paul said, "For I am convinced that neither death, nor life, nor angels, nor principalities, nor things present, nor things to come, nor powers, nor height, nor depth, nor any other created thing, will be able to separate us from the love of God, which is in Christ Jesus our Lord" (Romans 8:38-39). If you have been led to a wilderness, prepare for a new view of God's love.

When David realized God's lovingkindness was better than life, he was moved to praise God. Today ask the Lord to give you the ability to praise Him in the wilderness.

READ AND STUDY GOD'S WORD

1. Read David's words in Psalm 63:2-5 and describe David's expression of praise in the dry and weary land.

2. What can you know about God's love that will give you reason to praise even in your wilderness? Look at the following verses and write what you learn about God and His love:

John 3:16

Romans 5:3-8

Ephesians 3:16-19

1 John 4:10

3. God promises triumph in your testing. Read the following verses and underline the phrases that are most significant to you:

"For momentary, light affliction is producing for us an eternal weight of glory far beyond all comparison" (2 Corinthians 4:17).

"Consider it all joy, my brethren, when you encounter various trials, knowing that the testing of your faith produces endurance. And let endurance have its perfect result, so that you may be perfect and complete, lacking in nothing" (James 1:2-4).

ADORE GOD IN PRAYER

Talk with God about His love for you and the results of trials. Find reasons in the verses above to praise and worship God today.

YIELD YOURSELF TO GOD

Why yield to gloomy anticipations? Who told thee that the night would never end in day? Who told thee that the sea of circumstances would ebb out till there should be nothing left but long leagues of the mud of horrible poverty? Who told thee that the winter of thy discontent would proceed from frost to frost, from snow, and ice, and hail, to deeper snow, and yet more heavy tempest of despair? Knowest thou not that day follows night, that flood comes after ebb, that spring and summer succeed winter? Hope thou then! Hope thou ever! For God fails thee not. Dost thou not know that thy God loves thee in the midst of all this? Mountains, when in darkness hidden, are as real as in day, and God's love is as true to thee now as it was in thy brightest moments. No father chastens always: thy Lord hates the rod as much as thou dost; he only cares to use it for that reason which should make thee willing to receive it, namely, that it works thy lasting good. Thou shalt yet climb Jacob's ladder with the angels, and behold him who sits at the top of it—thy covenant God. Thou shalt yet, amidst the splendours of eternity, forget the trials of time, or only remember them to bless the God who led thee through them, and wrought thy lasting good by them. Come, sing in the midst of tribulation. Rejoice even while passing through the furnace. Make the wilderness to blossom like the rose! Cause the desert to ring with thine exulting joys, for these light afflictions will soon be over, and then "for ever with the Lord," thy bliss shall never wane.[5]

CHARLES SPURGEON

ENJOY HIS PRESENCE

What is the most important truth you have learned today about praising God in the wilderness?

Faint not nor fear, his arms are near,
He changeth not, and thou art dear;
Only believe and thou shalt see,
That Christ is all in all to thee.[6]

CHARLES SPURGEON

REST IN HIS LOVE

"In this is love, not that we loved God, but that He loved us and sent His Son to be the propitiation for our sins" (1 John 4:10).

REMEMBER HIM IN THE WILDERNESS

> *When I remember You on my bed,*
> *I meditate on You in the night watches,*
> *For You have been my help,*
> *And in the shadow of Your wings I sing for joy.*
> PSALM 63:6-7

PREPARE YOUR HEART

When you are in the wilderness, you will have some sleepless nights. Those nights can be the most intimate times with your Lord. Learn to think about Him in the night, and you will walk with Him in the day. Ask the Lord now to quiet your heart that you might hear Him speak in His Word.

READ AND STUDY GOD'S WORD

1. Read the following translations of Psalm 63:6-7 and underline your favorite words and phrases.

"When I remember You on my bed, I meditate on You in the night watches, for You have been my help, and in the shadow of Your wings I sing for joy."

"I remember you while I'm lying in bed; I think about you through the night. You are my help. Because of your protection, I sing" (NCV).

"If I'm sleepless at midnight, I spend the hours in grateful reflection. Because you've always stood up for me, I'm free to run and play" (MSG).

2. The sons of Korah wrote a wilderness song, and they also mention the beauty of the night. Read Psalm 42 and record what you can learn to help you when you are thirsty for the Lord.

ADORE GOD IN PRAYER

Using the words of Psalm 42, talk with God, remembering the truths that give you hope and encouragement.

YIELD YOURSELF TO GOD

> To desire God is to have him. To long for him is to be at the wellhead. To remember him on the bed rests us. To meditate on him in the night is to have the dawn. The shadow of his wings is absolute safety.[7]
>
> F.B. MEYER

ENJOY HIS PRESENCE

Can you see the value of remembering the Lord at night? Close your time with God today by writing a prayer to Him expressing all that is on your heart.

REST IN HIS LOVE

"The LORD will command His lovingkindness in the daytime, and His song will be with me in the night, a prayer to the God of my life" (Psalm 42:8).

CLING TO HIM IN THE WILDERNESS

My soul clings to You; Your right hand upholds me.

PSALM 63:8

PREPARE YOUR HEART

An anchored boat is held firmly in place regardless of the winds that attempt to shake it from its moorings. The hot desert wind can be fierce at times. However, when you cling to Him, you will stand strong, even in the wilderness. Begin your quiet time by meditating and praying through this poem by Gerhard Tersteegen:

> Draw me to Thee, till far within Thy rest,
> In stillness of Thy peace, Thy voice I hear—
> For ever quieted upon Thy breast,
> So loved, so near.
>
> By mystery of Thy touch my spirit thrilled,
> O Magnet all Divine;
> The hunger of my soul for ever stilled,
> For Thou art mine.
>
> For me, O Lord, the world is all too small,
> For I have seen Thy face,
> Where Thine eternal love irradiates all
> Within Thy secret place.
>
> And therefore from all others, from all else,
> Draw Thou my soul to Thee…
> …Yea—Thou hast broken the enchanter's spells,
> And I am free.

Now in the haven of untroubled rest
I land at last,
The hunger, and the thirst, and weary quest
For ever past.

There, Lord, to lose, in bliss of Thine embrace
The recreant will;
There, in the radiance of Thy blessed Face,
Be hushed and still.

There, speechless at Thy pierced Feet
See none and nought beside,
And know but this—that Thou art sweet,
That I am satisfied.[8]

READ AND STUDY GOD'S WORD

1. When you are in the wilderness, clinging to the Lord is your most important priority. Read the following translations of Psalm 63:8 and underline your favorite words and phrases.

"My soul clings to You; Your right hand upholds me."

"I stay close to you; you support me with your right hand" (NCV).

"My soul follows close behind You; Your right hand upholds me" (NKJV).

"I cling to you; your strong right hand holds me securely" (NLT).

"My whole being follows hard after You and clings closely to You; Your right hand upholds me" (AMP).

"I hold on to you for dear life, and you hold me steady as a post" (MSG).

2. The Hebrew word translated "cling" is *dabaq* and means to stay close to someone. In Psalm 63:8, it shows us that we are to stay close to the Lord. This will include affection, loyalty, obedience, faithfulness, and walking in His ways. Read the following verses and write what you learn about clinging to the Lord:

Deuteronomy 13:4

Joshua 23:8-11

2 Kings 18:1-6

3. The Lord often used Jeremiah, His prophet, as an object lesson for the people of Israel. God's people had betrayed Him by worshipping idols. Their sinful actions broke His heart. Read Jeremiah 13:1-11 and write your insights about how the waistband demonstrates the kind of relationship the Lord desires with His people.

ADORE GOD IN PRAYER

Be not far from me, O Lord, this day; and through all its hours may I be found doing those things that are pleasing in your sight. May I, like Enoch, walk with God and, like him, have the testimony that I please God.[9]

F.B. MEYER

YIELD YOURSELF TO GOD

Real desolation is distance from God. This anguish the righteous soul cannot endure. With every energy, with every power, it presses after its beloved object. It seeks uninterrupted fellowship. But ah! How often is it weak to follow—how often do the tottering limbs need to be upheld! This help is very near. God extends His right hand, and thus the fainting one pursues his course. Divine help enables to draw nigh to God, and to reach the presence which is heaven begun.[10]

HENRY LAW

ENJOY HIS PRESENCE

As you think about all you have learned today about clinging to the Lord, describe the kind of relationship the Lord desires with you. How will such a relationship with God help you in the wilderness experiences of life?

REST IN HIS LOVE

"You shall follow the LORD your God and fear Him; and you shall keep His commandments, listen to His voice, serve Him, and cling to Him" (Deuteronomy 13:4).

GLORIFY HIM IN THE WILDERNESS

But the king will rejoice in God;
Everyone who swears by Him will glory,
For the mouths of those who speak lies will be stopped.
PSALM 63:11

PREPARE YOUR HEART

Sometimes God places His choice servants in dry and weary lands where there is no water. David was described as the man after God's own heart, and even he was in just such a place. The wilderness is a place of testing and also a place of triumph. When you praise God, remember Him, and cling to Him, as David did, you discover views of God not seen elsewhere. Such beauty gives you joy—not the absence of suffering, but the presence of God Himself. When God is present, He lights up any dark place. Ultimately, your journey in the wilderness brings God great glory. Others watch what God is doing in your life. They stand in awe as God does what only He can do—only He can give you cause to praise in sadness, only He can give you the ability to look at Him in His Word, and only He can give you the strength to hold on to Him and not give up. And then, they bend the knee, worship God, and give Him glory. You have what the world wishes for—unshakeable, untouchable glory—the very glory of God through Christ's indwelling presence, made possible by the Holy Spirit (2 Corinthians 3:18; 4:6). This treasure is, as Paul says, "in earthen vessels, so that the surpassing greatness of the power will be of God and not from ourselves" (2 Corinthians 4:7).

God explains the purpose of the wilderness experience in Isaiah 41:20 when He says, "That they may see and recognize, and consider and gain insight as well, that the hand of the LORD has done this, and the Holy One of Israel has created it." Others are watching those in the wilderness. And as He opens rivers on the bare heights and springs in the midst of valleys, makes the wilderness a pool of water, and causes fountains to flow on the dry lands, He gets all the glory. For He does what no man can do. And He will cause such reviving waters to flow through your life so that "times of refreshing may come from the presence of the Lord" (Acts 3:19). Therefore, never give up. David's experience can be your experience. In your prayers, learn the lessons of David in the wilderness—praise, remember, and cling to the Lord. When you do, you will bring great glory to your Father.

Draw near to the Lord this morning in your quiet time and pray, *Lord, will You glorify Yourself in my life in the wilderness experiences, where I am often thirsty? Strengthen me to praise, cause me to remember, and help me cling to You.*

READ AND STUDY GOD'S WORD

1. Today, on your last day in Psalm 63 in this quiet time experience, read through the words of this psalm again and write out your most significant insight. One of the beauties of God's Word is its freshness each day. What you read yesterday will be new for today.

2. Notice these words of David: "The king will rejoice in God; everyone who swears by Him will glory" (Psalm 63:11). The Hebrew word translated "glory" is *halal* and means to shine. God's presence brings light to the wilderness and light to your life—He will cause you to shine with His beauty and radiance. Read the following verses and write out what you learn about glory:

Psalm 3:3

Psalm 19:1

Psalm 24:7-8

Psalm 84:11

Psalm 138:5-8

2 Corinthians 3:18

2 Corinthians 4:6-7

ADORE GOD IN PRAYER

Take some time to look through your prayer pages in the back of this book. How has God answered your prayers? How is He working in your life? Write out any new requests to take before Him now. Then thank Him and praise Him for His presence in your life.

YIELD YOURSELF TO GOD

Amid external desolations inward joy can be abundant. The wilderness and the solitary place shall be glad; the desert shall rejoice and blossom as the rose. The Lord will make the wilderness a pool of water and the dry land springs of water. He will plant in the wilderness the choicest of evergreens. As the body craves the support of food, so too the soul has craving appetites. But they are all satisfied. The manna falls and gives support and strength. The pilgrim sits down beneath the tree of life. Its laden branches present refreshing produce. The fruit is sweet to the taste. They who hunger and thirst after God assuredly shall be filled. The richest fruit is ever by their side. When evening shades prevail, the inward light does not expire. When the body needs repose, the active mind will hold communion with the Lord, and the night-watches be calmed with heavenly meditations. Experience recalls past help. The soul nestles beneath the shadow of God's wings and is right glad.[11]

HENRY LAW

ENJOY HIS PRESENCE

What have you learned over this last week that helps you in the wilderness experiences of life? Close by writing a prayer to the Lord, expressing all that is on your heart today.

They who seek the throne of grace
Find that throne in every place;
If we live a life of prayer,
God is present everywhere.

In our sickness and our health,
In our want, or in our wealth,
If we look to God in prayer,
God is present everywhere.

When our earthly comforts fail,
When the woes of life prevail,
'Tis the time for earnest prayer;
God is present everywhere.

Then, my soul, in every strait,
To thy Father come, and wait;
He will answer every prayer:
God is present everywhere.[12]

OLIVER HOLDEN

REST IN HIS LOVE

"And they will sing of the ways of the LORD, for great is the glory of the LORD" (Psalm 138:5).

DEVOTIONAL READING
BY JAMES H. McCONKEY

Prayer is the passage-way from spiritual thirst to spiritual refreshing…Some know only the thirst, only the distress, because they use not the way out of both—the *cry*. God does not mean us to live in a permanent state of need or a permanent condition of distress, but out of the need and out of the distress to cry and have a well opened…Who is there, buffeted, dispirited, weary unto death, who has not cried unto Him in their distress and, in the quiet inflow of peace, comfort, and rest, been as conscious that He had opened a stream of refreshing in their souls as though their ears heard its musical flow, their parched lips tasted its sweet running waters.[13]

Take some time now to write about all that you have learned this week. What has been most significant to you? Close by writing a prayer to the Lord.

PRAYER WHEN YOU WANT TO GO HIGHER

PSALM 130

Real prayer at its highest and best reveals a soul athirst for God—just for God alone. Real prayer comes from the lips of those whose affection is set on things above.

THE KNEELING CHRISTIAN

PRAYER FROM THE DEPTHS TO THE HEIGHTS

Out of the depths I have cried to You, O LORD.

PSALM 130:1

PREPARE YOUR HEART

We are pilgrims on a pilgrimage. The pilgrimage perspective is written all over the Bible and especially in the psalms (see Psalm 84:5). Christians have the distinct privilege of being men and women of whom this world is not worthy, roughly treated at times, and even suffering emotional pain throughout their lives. Yet through God's divine empowerment through the Holy Spirit, the Lord's pilgrims are enabled to look beyond the temporal to the eternal. Their eternal home is just beyond the mist, past the dim mirror of this world. Prayer can take us into the realm of glory, power, and a new perspective any moment of the day. Watchman Nee says, "Our prayers lay the track down on which God's power can come. Like a mighty locomotive, his power is irresistible, but it cannot reach us without rails."[1] When we learn to travel the road of passionate prayer—prayer from the heart—we are taken from earth to heaven. The psalmists knew these truths and wrote often about them. One group of psalms in particular uniquely carry you on the heavenly journey—the Psalms of Ascent or the Book of Pilgrim Songs—Psalms 120–134. These psalms are considered to be pilgrim songs for going up from one's dwelling place to Jerusalem for the three major feasts.[2] Joseph and Mary may have sung these songs when they went to Jerusalem with the young Jesus (Luke 2:41). Jesus could have sung these psalms as He journeyed to Jerusalem with His disciples.

The Psalms of Ascent show us that we can go higher when we are in trials and also when our life seems routine and every day seems the same. The psalmists teach us how. You will notice that such saints as Amy Carmichael and A.W. Tozer knew these secrets, for they had spent much time with God in His Word. You never want to settle for an earthly perspective, but instead want to always go higher with the Lord. Like Habakkuk, you will be able to say, "Though the fig tree should not blossom and there be no fruit on the vines, though the yield of the olive should fail and the fields produce no food, though the flock should be cut off from the fold and there be no cattle in the stalls, yet I will exult in the LORD, I will rejoice in the God of my salvation. The Lord

GOD is my strength, and He has made my feet like hinds' feet, and makes me walk on my high places" (Habakkuk 3:17-19). Today, ask the Lord to teach you the prayer to take you higher with Him into the eternal realm of His glory and grace.

READ AND STUDY GOD'S WORD

1. In our quiet times this week we are going to meditate on the words of Psalm 130, the song of ascent taking us from the depths to the heights through supplication, grace, waiting, and hope. We do not know the author of this psalm, but we can understand some of his life challenges through the words he writes. Read Psalm 130 and write out what you observe about the author.

2. Clearly the author of this psalm knows the experience of the depths, those times when there seems little reason for hope and no way out of one's circumstance. These are the deep waters of trials and oppressions. Others in the Bible knew the depths. Read the following verses and write out what you learn about their experience in the depths:

Psalm 42:7

Psalm 69:2

Lamentations 3:48-55

3. The psalmist knows the answer for such trials, "Out of the depths, I have cried to You, O LORD. Lord, hear my voice" (Psalm 130:1-2). Crying out to the Lord is your great answer in the depths of a difficulty—it is the prayer when you want to "go higher" with the Lord. Those who wrote Psalms 42 and 69 and Lamentations knew this answer as well. Read the following verses and underline the words and phrases that are most significant to you today:

"The LORD will command His lovingkindness in the daytime; and His song will be with me in the night, a prayer to the God of my life" (Psalm 42:8).

"But as for me, my prayer is to You, O LORD, at an acceptable time; O God, in the greatness of Your lovingkindness, answer me with Your saving truth. Deliver me from the mire and do not let me sink; may I be delivered from my foes and from the deep waters. May the flood of water not overflow me nor the deep swallow me up, nor the pit shut its mouth on me. Answer me, O LORD, for Your lovingkindness is good; according to the greatness of Your compassion, turn to me, And do not hide Your face from Your servant, for I am in distress; answer me quickly" (Psalm 69:13-16).

"I called on Your name, O LORD, out of the lowest pit. You have heard my voice, do not hide Your ear from my prayer for relief, from my cry for help. You drew near when I called on You; You said, 'Do not fear!'" (Lamentations 3:55-57).

ADORE GOD IN PRAYER

Come near, O our God, come nearer, nearer, nearer. Still some secret to our heart reveal, as yet undiscovered. Thou hast led some of us into darkness and not into light, and Thou hast covered us in the night watches and made it darkness round about us, till our spirit sank within us. Now it is Thy way to bring light out of darkness, and joy out of sorrow…

O Lord, Thy people want this; nothing can so strengthen, comfort, lighten, sanctify and perfect us as this. Are we earth bound? Oh, for Thy presence, and we shall be of heavenly mind. Are we deeply depressed in spirit? Oh, for the light of Thy countenance, for it shall make us gladder than a wedding day. Oh, that we might get at Thee, our God, for then shall the bonds of this world seem like cobwebs and disappear.[3]

CHARLES SPURGEON

YIELD YOURSELF TO GOD

Trial quickens us in prayer, and so effectually helps us heavenward. The life of God in the soul on earth is a life of communion of the soul with God in heaven. Prayer is nothing less than the divine nature in fellowship with the divine, the renewed creature in communion with God. And it would be as impossible for a regenerate soul to live without prayer, as for the natural life to exist without breathing. Oh, what a sacred and precious privilege is this! Is there one compared with it? When we have closed the door—for we speak now of that most solemn and holy habit of prayer, private communion—and have shut out the world, and the creature, and even the saints, and are closeted in personal, solemn, and confiding audience with God, what words can portray the preciousness and solemnity of that hour! Then is guilt confessed, and backslidings deplored, and care unburdened, and sorrow unveiled, and pardon sought, and grace implored, and blessings invoked…There is no ladder, the rungs of which will bring you so near to God, there are no wings the plumage of which will carry you so close to heaven as prayer. The moment you have unpinioned your soul for communion with God, let your pressure, your sorrow, your sin be what it may, that moment your heart has departed earth and is on its way heavenward. You are soaring above the region of sorrow and battle and sin, and your spirit is expatiating beneath a purer, happier, sunnier sky. Oh the soothing, the strengthening, the uplifting found in prayer beneath the cross! Thus trial helps us heavenward by quickening us to devotion, by stirring us up to closeness of walk.[4]

OCTAVIUS WINSLOW

ENJOY HIS PRESENCE

Can you think of a time when the Lord pulled you out of the depths and set you on higher ground? How do you need the Lord to take you higher today? Write a prayer to Him, expressing all that is on your heart.

REST IN HIS LOVE

"Waters flowed over my head; I said, 'I am cut off!' I called on Your name, O LORD, out of the lowest pit. You have heard my voice" (Lamentations 3:54-56).

THE PRAYER OF SUPPLICATION

LORD, hear my voice!
Let Your ears be attentive to the voice of my supplications.
PSALM 130:2

PREPARE YOUR HEART

God hears your prayers and will answer. He promises. The psalmists relied on God's response to their cries, and you can rely on Him for His answer.

A woman in England resolved to pray for the conversion of her unsaved husband for 12 months. At noon every day, she went to her room and cried out to God for her husband. Her husband was too antagonistic about spiritual matters to even talk about God. The 12 months passed with seemingly no results.

She decided to pray for six months longer in the same way as before. And again, after six months, there was still no change in her husband. And so, she asked herself, *Can I give up on him?* The Lord brought her to a new and deeper prayer commitment. *No, I will pray for him as long as God gives me breath.*

That very day, when he came home, instead of going to the dining room for dinner, he went upstairs. She waited and waited. He never came down to dinner. Finally she went upstairs to check on her husband. She found him on his knees crying out to God to have mercy on him. He was convicted of his sin and became a Christian and a committed student of the Bible. God answered the prayers of a wife who was willing to pray in spite of no apparent immediate result.

Today in your quiet time, ask God to teach you the prayer of supplication, taking you from the depth of a need to the height of His answer.

READ AND STUDY GOD'S WORD

1. Today you are going to look at one kind of prayer the psalmist prayed when he was in the depths—the prayer of supplication. The Hebrew word translated "supplication" is *tahanun* and denotes a prayer for favor and mercy related to a particular need or circumstance. The Greek word translated "supplication" is *deesis* and means to make known a particular need for yourself or someone else. When you make a supplication, you are praying to the one who can help

you—God. Supplications aren't general, they're specific, detailed requests. Read Psalm 130:2 and write out everything you learn about supplication. ("Supplication" is translated "prayer" in the NLT.)

2. Read through Psalm 130 again. What was the theme of the psalmist's supplication? What did he want from the Lord?

3. The Bible gives many examples of those who made prayers and supplications (also translated "petitions") to the Lord. Read the following verses and write out what you learn about how to pray a prayer of supplication.

1 Kings 8:52-54

Daniel 9:2-3

Philippians 4:6-7

Hebrews 5:7

ADORE GOD IN PRAYER

Where in your life today do you need to ask God for His favor and mercy? Devote a prayer page to your needs. Be specific, date each request, and watch expectantly to see what God will do (Psalm 5:3).

YIELD YOURSELF TO GOD

We must be pre-eminently people of prayer. Our hearts must graduate in the school of prayer, for only in the school of prayer can the heart learn to minister. No learning can make up for the failure to pray. No earnestness, no diligence, no study will supply its lack. Talking to others for God is a great thing. But talking to God for others is greater still. We will never speak to people for God with real success until we have learned how to speak to God for people.[5]

E.M. BOUNDS

I tell you, the man who lives with God in *little matters*—who walks with God in the minutiae of his life—is the man who becomes the best acquainted with God—with His character, His faithfulness, His love. To meet God in my daily trials, to take to Him the trials of my calling, the trials of my church, the trials of my family, the trials of my own heart; to take to Him that which brings the shadow upon my brow, that rends the sigh from my heart—to remember it is not too trivial to take to God—above all, to take to Him the least taint upon the conscience, the slightest pressure of sin upon the heart, the softest conviction of departure from God—to take it to Him, and confess it at the foot of the cross, with the hand of faith upon the bleeding sacrifice—oh! these are the paths in which a man becomes intimately and closely acquainted with God.[6]

OCTAVIUS WINSLOW

ENJOY HIS PRESENCE

Have you learned to take all your needs to the Lord in prayer? The psalmists were well versed in praying to God about the little matters Octavius Winslow spoke of and about the deep trials of the soul. What is the most important truth you have learned in your quiet time today that will motivate you to pray?

REST IN HIS LOVE

"So I gave my attention to the Lord God to seek Him by prayer and supplications, with fasting, sackcloth and ashes" (Daniel 9:3).

THE PRAYER BECAUSE OF GRACE

If You, LORD, should mark iniquities, O Lord, who could stand?
But there is forgiveness with You, that You may be feared.

PSALM 130:3-4

PREPARE YOUR HEART

When you want to climb to the heights with your Lord, you become more and more aware of your own unworthiness. The greatness of God is both humbling and exhilarating. It's humbling because you see a holy God, and it's exhilarating because you experience a personal and loving God. This great God has called you to engage in the great adventure of knowing Him. But how can you know Him when you have clearly sinned against Him? This is how: He has cleared the way for your sins to be forgiven by paying the penalty for your sin. The love story of grace—God's unmerited favor and unconditional love—is told throughout the Bible. Even those in the Old Testament knew the grace of God. The psalmist said, "If You, LORD, should mark iniquities, O Lord, who could stand? But there is forgiveness with You, that You may be feared" (Psalm 130:3-4).

John Wesley was riding through the countryside one day on his preaching circuit. He was attacked by thieves who stole all his money. He wrote the following prayer in his journal that night: "Dear God, thank you for 3 things: tho' they took my money, they didn't take my life... tho' they took ALL my money, it wasn't much...most of all, thank you that it was I who was robbed, and not I who did the robbing!" John Wesley realized the truth behind the saying, "There but for the grace of God go I." To go higher with the Lord, we must realize we are sinners saved by grace. The security and freedom granted to you by God's grace gives you the boldness to dare to intimately know your God.

Today, ask God to give you a deep knowledge of His magnificent grace.

READ AND STUDY GOD'S WORD

1. Martin Luther called certain psalms the Pauline Psalms because they contain truths about the grace and forgiveness of God.[7] Psalm 130 is one of those Pauline Psalms because of its view of

God as a forgiving, gracious God. Read the following translations of Psalm 130:3-4 and underline the words and phrases that help you understand God's grace and forgiveness.

> "If You, LORD, should mark iniquities, O Lord, who could stand? But there is forgiveness with You, that You may be feared."

> "If you, O LORD, kept a record of sins, O Lord, who could stand? But with you there is forgiveness; therefore you are feared" (NIV).

> "LORD, if you kept a record of our sins, who, O Lord, could ever survive? But you offer forgiveness, that we might learn to fear you" (NLT).

> "If You, Lord, should keep account of and treat [us according to our] sins, O Lord, who could stand? [Ps. 143:2, Rom. 3:20, Gal. 2:16.] But there is forgiveness with You [just what man needs], that You may be reverently feared and worshiped [Deut. 10:12.]" (AMP).

2. Grace is your great encouragement to pray. Read the following verses and write out what you learn about grace that will help you in your prayers to the Lord:

Psalm 84:11

Romans 5:1-2,15-17

2 Corinthians 9:8

Ephesians 2:8

Hebrews 4:16

James 4:6

2 Peter 3:18

3. What is the most important truth you have learned about the grace of God from your study in the Word?

ADORE GOD IN PRAYER

Thank the Lord today for His magnificent grace and forgiveness, naming each way you have seen Him express these gifts in your own life.

YIELD YOURSELF TO GOD

A blessed change takes place in the sinner's state, when he becomes a true believer, whatever he has been. Being justified by faith he has peace with God. The holy, righteous God, cannot be at peace with a sinner, while under the guilt of sin. Justification takes away the guilt, and so makes way for peace. This is through our Lord Jesus Christ; through him as the great Peace-maker, the Mediator between God and man. The saints' happy state is a state of grace.[8]

MATTHEW HENRY

ENJOY HIS PRESENCE

What does the forgiveness and grace of God mean to you today? How does knowing you are forgiven and a recipient of His grace help you in your prayer to know Him more?

Sweet is the precious gift of prayer,
To bow before a throne of grace;
To leave our every burden there,
And gain new strength to run our race;
To gird our heavenly armor on,
Depending on the Lord alone.

And sweet the whisper of His love,
When conscience sinks beneath its load,
That bids our guilty fears remove,
And points to Christ's atoning blood;
Oh, then 'tis sweet indeed to know
God can be just and gracious too.

But oh, to see our Savior's face!
From sin and sorrow to be freed!
To dwell in His divine embrace—
This will be sweeter far indeed!
The fairest form of earthly bliss
Is less than nought, compared with this.[9]

REST IN HIS LOVE

"Therefore let us draw near with confidence to the throne of grace, so that we may receive mercy and find grace to help in time of need" (Hebrews 4:16).

THE PRAYER OF WAITING

My soul waits for the Lord more than the watchmen for the morning;
Indeed, more than the watchmen for the morning.
PSALM 130:6

PREPARE YOUR HEART

One of the happy truths of the Christian life is that the dark roads are not without purpose, but weave into God's grand design. We can confidently walk on, faithfully following our Lord. Though we know not where we are going, we know God has a plan and we can count on it. Some roads require a patient waiting until God brings us out into that broad place where we see what He was up to from the first. Waiting is imperative in the prayer that takes us higher with the Lord. Some of the most magnificent vistas are reached only through the most treacherous passages. So, dear friend, as you go on with the Lord this day, draw near to Him and ask Him to give you a deep trust and willingness to wait on Him.

READ AND STUDY GOD'S WORD

1. When your life comes to a standstill, you are forced to do what never seems to come naturally—wait. The psalmists often spoke of the need to wait and of their own willingness to wait. When you study their words about waiting, you see how God helped them to do what they could never do alone. Read Psalm 130:5-6 and write everything you learn about waiting.

2. Notice that the psalmist waited as watchmen wait for the morning. Yours is a waiting that watches, like one who is up all night knowing that the sun will indeed eventually rise. George MacDonald encourages you to "get up early and go to the mountain and watch God make a morning. The dull gray will give way as God pushes the sun towards the horizon, and there will be tints and hues of every shade, that will blend into one perfect light as the full-orbed sun bursts into view."[10] Herein is the picture of waiting—as a watchman for the morning. A good way to

remember the meaning of waiting is the acrostic WAIT—Watching, Always I Trust. Have you learned this kind of waiting? Read the following verses and write out what you learn about waiting on God:

Psalm 25:4-5

Psalm 27:14

Psalm 37:7-9

Psalm 40:1-2

3. Moses knew how to wait on God. Read these words from his psalm, Psalm 90:12-17, and write out those prayers that will help you wait today.

ADORE GOD IN PRAYER

Heavenly Father, I know assuredly that all things are working together for my good, but help me to wait patiently and toil diligently, though the waiting be long and the toil hard.[11]

F.B. MEYER

YIELD YOURSELF TO GOD

A holy, joyful expectancy is of the very essence of true waiting. And this is not only true in reference to the many varied requests every believer has to make, but most especially to the one great petition which ought to be the chief thing every heart seeks for itself—that the life of God in the soul may have full sway. That Christ may be fully formed within, and that we may be filled to all the fullness of God. This is what God has promised. This is what God's people too little seek, very often because they do not believe it possible. This is what we ought to seek and dare to expect, because God is able and waiting to work it in us. But, God Himself must work it. And for this end our working must cease. We must see how entirely it is to be the faith of the operation of God who raised Jesus from the dead—just as much as the resurrection, the perfecting of God's life in our souls is to be directly His work. And, waiting has to become, more than ever a tarrying before God in stillness of soul, counting upon Him who raises the dead and calls the things that not as though they were…the one thing I have to do is this: to look to the Lord; to wait for the God of my salvation; to hold fast the confident assurance, "My God will hear me."[12]

ANDREW MURRAY

The time that we are kept waiting seems long, but the happy result will enable us to reflect upon the time as short, as but a moment. It is no longer than God has appointed, and we are sure His time is the best time and His favors are worth waiting for. The time is long, but it is nothing compared with the days of eternity, when those who had great patience will be recompensed for it with an everlasting salvation. Though it is a dark day, let us wait on God all the day. Even though, while we are kept waiting for what God will do, we are kept in the dark concerning what He is doing and what is best for us to do, let us be content to wait in the dark. Though we do not see any signs, though there is no one to tell us how long, let us resolve to wait, however long it may be. For though we do not know right now what God is doing, we will know hereafter, when the mystery of God is finished.[13]

MATTHEW HENRY

ENJOY HIS PRESENCE

Are you willing to wait for God's highest and best in your life today? Perhaps something is pressing in on you, challenging your faith and tempting you to give up. Dear friend, hang on to what you know is true in God's Word. He is bringing His purposes to pass though you may not see it now. You may need to identify with the psalmist of Psalm 130 today and become as the watchmen who wait for the morning. You can know that indeed the sun will rise at the given time prescribed by your Lord. And indeed, there is the great sunrise of eternity that will be yours to enjoy forever.

> We are too apt to wait for circumstances, people, things, and to meet with disappointment, because they are apart from Himself. But those who wait for the Lord cannot be ashamed. There may be no Theophany, but, as they wait, a new strength and comfort steal into their hearts. Oh to have the eagerness of the watcher for the dawn, as we wait for God! And should not we all cherish this expectancy for the breaking of that eternal morning, when the day shall dawn on which night never falls?[14]
>
> F.B. MEYER

> He writes in characters too grand
> For our short sight to understand;
> We catch but broken strokes, and try
> To fathom all the mystery
> Of withered hopes, of death, of life,
> The endless war, the useless strife,—
> But there, with larger, clearer sight,
> We shall see this—His way was right.[15]
>
> JOHN OXENHAM

REST IN HIS LOVE

"Rest in the LORD and wait patiently for Him" (Psalm 37:7).

THE PRAYER OF HOPE

O Israel, hope in the LORD;
For with the LORD there is lovingkindness,
And with Him is abundant redemption.

PSALM 130:7

PREPARE YOUR HEART

As we near the end of these quiet times on passionate prayer in the psalms, we have learned how to adore God, confess sin, thank and praise Him, and pray to go higher and deeper in our relationship with our Lord. The psalmists have been our prayer partners, teaching us and helping us experience our God in a deeper way.

Will you take some time now, reflecting on all you have learned even this week, and thank the Lord for His presence in your life? You can always know that the Lord is with you. And because He is here, you are never alone, and you always have hope. Even when you think you are without hope, hope remains. In God's economy, He can do what no man can do, and with Him all things are possible. Is this just wishful thinking? No. He promises His faithfulness and strength to you, and He is worthy of your greatest trust. So hang on, even if by a thread, for He will fulfill every promise He makes to you in His Word. Paul says, "For as many as are the promises of God, in Him they are yes; therefore also through Him is our Amen to the glory of God through us" (2 Corinthians 1:20). Another translation expresses the words this way, "The yes to all of God's promises is in Christ" (NCV). Because of Jesus, you can hang on to God's promises, trust in His words, and cry out a resounding "Yes! Thank You, Lord, for Your faithfulness."

READ AND STUDY GOD'S WORD

1. Today, in your quiet time, you are going to focus on hope in the promises of God. You will notice in your reading of Psalm 130 that the psalmist knew how to have hope. Read Psalm 130 and write out what you learn about hope.

2. The psalmist's hope was in God and His Word—"in His word do I hope" (verse 5), and "hope in the LORD" (verse 7). You can always remember the meaning of hope with this acrostic—HOPE is Holding On with Patient Expectation. And what are you holding on to? The promises of God in His Word. Read Psalm 130 again and write out all the promises of God—those truths that were important to the psalmist in his difficulty.

3. Always ask the Lord to give you His promise to hold on to so you may have hope. Read the following verses on hope, underlining your favorite words and verses.

"Be strong and let your heart take courage, all you who hope in the LORD" (Psalm 31:24).

"But as for me, I will hope continually, and will praise You yet more and more" (Psalm 71:14).

"Remember Your word to Your servant, in which You have made me hope. This is my comfort in my affliction, that Your word has revived me" (Psalm 119:49-50).

"The hope of the righteous is gladness, but the expectation of the wicked perishes" (Proverbs 10:28).

"'For I know the plans that I have for you,' declares the LORD, 'plans for welfare and not for calamity to give you a future and a hope'" (Jeremiah 29:11).

"'The Lord is my portion,' says my soul, 'Therefore I have hope in Him.' The LORD is good to those who wait for Him, to the person who seeks Him" (Lamentations 3:24-25).

"In hope against hope he [Abraham] believed, so that he might become a father of many nations according to that which had been spoken, 'So shall your descendants be'" (Romans 4:18).

"For whatever was written in earlier times was written for our instruction, so that through perseverance and the encouragement of the Scriptures we might have hope" (Romans 15:4).

"Now may the God of hope fill you with all joy and peace in believing, so that you will abound in hope by the power of the Holy Spirit" (Romans 15:13).

4. What are the most important truths you have learned about hope? How will hope help you in your life of prayer?

ADORE GOD IN PRAYER

Now that you have spent a week in Psalm 130, take some time and pray through the words of this Psalm of Ascent, which takes you higher in your relationship with your Lord. Direct each phrase to Him.

YIELD YOURSELF TO GOD

> O child of suffering, be thou patient; God has not passed thee over in his providence. He who is the feeder of sparrows, will also furnish you with what you need. Sit not down in despair; hope on, hope ever. Take up the arms of faith against a sea of trouble, and your opposition shall yet end your distresses. There is One who careth for you. His eye is fixed on you, his heart beats with pity for your woe, and his hand omnipotent shall yet bring you the needed help. The darkest cloud shall scatter itself in showers of mercy. The blackest gloom shall give place to the morning. He, if thou art one of his family, will bind up thy wounds, and heal thy broken heart. Doubt not his grace because of thy tribulation, but believe that he loveth thee as much in seasons of trouble as in times of happiness. What a serene and quiet life might you lead if you would leave providing to the God of providence! With a little oil in the cruse, and a handful of meal in the barrel, Elijah outlived the famine, and you will do the same. If God cares for you, why need you care too? Can you trust him for your soul, and not for your body? He has never refused to bear your burdens, he has never fainted under their weight. Come, then, soul! have done with fretful care, and leave all thy concerns in the hand of a gracious God.[16]
>
> CHARLES SPURGEON

ENJOY HIS PRESENCE

Think about all you have learned throughout this quiet time experience in the psalms with the psalmists as your personal prayer partners. The Lord has given you these faithful writers to accompany you and help you pray along the way in your life journey. All you need to do is open your Bible to Psalms and pray the words. God is faithful to make His Word come alive and minister to your heart (Hebrews 4:12). You will find that His Word speaks to you when nothing else seems to help you. Sometimes you won't even realize how His Word is bringing healing to your heart and soul. But one day you will awaken to a new hope, a new joy, a new light in your eyes. And you will find the strength to go on.

Turn to the letter you wrote at the beginning of this study and read the words of your prayer to the Lord. How has God worked in your life? What have you learned? Close by writing a prayer, expressing all that is on your heart today. God bless you as you continue on in the great adventure of knowing Him.

All-loving Father, sometimes we have walked under starless skies that dripped darkness like drenching rain. We despaired of starshine or moonlight or sunrise. The sullen blackness gloomed above us as if it would last forever. And out of the dark there spoke no soothing voice to mend our broken hearts. We would gladly have welcomed some wild thunder peal to break the torturing stillness of that overbrooding night. But Thy winsome whisper of eternal love spoke more sweetly to our bruised and bleeding souls than any winds that breathe across Aeolian harps. It was Thy "still small voice" that spoke to us. We were listening and we heard. We looked and saw Thy face radiant with the light of love. And when we heard Thy voice and saw Thy face, new life came back to us as life comes back to whithered blooms that drink the summer rain.[17]

REST IN HIS LOVE

"Now may the God of hope fill you with all joy and peace in believing, so that you will abound in hope by the power of the Holy Spirit" (Romans 15:13).

DEVOTIONAL READING
BY OCTAVIUS WINSLOW

Our adorable Lord came down to earth to allure us up to heaven. In all his delineations of that happy, holy place, he sought to present it to the believing eye clad in its richest beauty and invested with its sweetest and most winning attractions. Its hope was to sanctify us, its prospect was to animate us, and its foretastes were to comfort us. Nothing, therefore, was wanting in the imagery with which he pictured its character and in the colouring with which he painted its glory to invite and attracts us to its peaceful, blissful coasts…

Transfer your thoughts, my reader, from the earthly to the heavenly—take the purest, the fondest, the most poetic conception you can form of the one, and blend it with the other—and still you have but the faintest analogy of heaven! And yet you have some approximation to the idea. You have entwined around your heart the image and hope of heaven as your home…

If now we are the children of God, then ours is not a state of dreary orphanage; we are not fatherless and homeless…

As you cross the desert sands, or break your lone footsteps through the depth of the wilderness, or stand within the sacred shadow of the cross, God is preparing you for the music-mansion of glory. All his dealings with you in providence and in grace are but to train and attune the powers, affections, and sympathies of your soul to the sweet harmony of the spheres. Every sunbeam of mercy that gilds your path, and every cloud-veil of judgment that shades it, every heavy footstep of the giant storm, every gentle wavelet dimpling the calm surface of the soul, every soft zephyr that lulls it to repose, is designed by God to instruct and mature you for the music of the celestial state. A harp of gold strung by angels and attuned by Christ's own hands awaits you in the music-mansion above and soon you will sweep its chords to the high praises of the triune Jehovah and all heaven will ring with its melody.[18]

Take some time now to write about all that you have learned this week and throughout this quiet time experience. What has been most significant to you? Close by writing a prayer to the Lord.

≈ DISCUSSION QUESTIONS ≈

INTRODUCTORY WEEK

Begin your class with prayer and then welcome everyone to this book of quiet times. Have the people in your group share their names and what brought them to the study. Make sure each person in your group has a book. Also, gather contact information for all participants in your group including name, address, phone number, and e-mail. That way you can keep in touch and encourage those in your group.

Familiarize your group with the layout of the book. Each week consists of five days of quiet times and devotional reading and response for days 6 and 7. Each day follows the PRAYER quiet time plan:

Prepare Your Heart

Read and Study God's Word

Adore God in Prayer

Yield Yourself to God

Enjoy His Presence

Rest in His Love

Journal and prayer pages are included in the back of the book. Note that the quiet times offer devotional reading, Bible study, prayer, and practical application.

You can determine how to organize your group sessions, but here's one idea: Discuss the week of quiet times together in the first hour, break for ten minutes, and then watch the message on the companion DVD. There are nine messages for this quiet time experience—one for the introduction and one for each week. You might also share with your group a summary of how to prepare for their quiet time by setting aside a time each day and a place. Consider sharing how time alone with the Lord has made a difference in your own life. Let your class know about the Quiet Time Ministries websites: www.quiettime.org and www.myquiettime.com.

You might want to type up a class schedule with the dates and titles of each week so those in your group can keep on track if they miss a week. This will also help them know when the class begins and ends. Some leaders like to divide the weeks up (completing the study in 16 weeks) by discussing days 1–3 one week and days 4–7 another week. This allows those in your group to journey through each quiet time at a slower pace. You may also want to use a visual aid such as a whiteboard to record some of the responses from your class on questions from the study.

Pray for one another by offering a way to record and exchange prayer requests. Some groups like to pass around a basket with cards that people can use to record prayer requests. Then, people take a request out of the basket and pray for someone during the week. Others like to use three by five cards and then exchange cards on a weekly basis.

Close this Introductory class with prayer, take a short break, and show the companion DVD message.

Week One: *Praying with the Psalmists*

DAY 1: The First Thing

Welcome everyone to this quiet time experience. In this first week you had the opportunity to look at the priority of prayer and the value of the psalms for your prayers.

1. What encouraged you most in the introduction?

2. What did you learn about the importance of prayer from your study in God's Word in day 1?

3. What was your favorite quote from your quiet time?

4. What would you like to see happen in your life of prayer as a result of this study?

DAY 2: Passionate About Prayer

1. In day 2 we thought about our passion for prayer. How was Jim Elliot an example of someone who was passionate about prayer? What stood out to you about his prayers?

2. How did the words of Psalm 30 show you the importance of prayer in David's life?

3. How did you see David's passion for prayer in his psalms?

DAY 3: Preoccupied with Praise

1. One of the outstanding qualities of the psalms is praise. What did you learn about praise in day 3?

2. What was your favorite part of the Puritan prayer in Prepare Your Heart?

3. How did Asaph teach you about praise in the verses you studied?

4. You had the opportunity to write some prayers of praise. What did you praise the Lord for this week?

DAY 4: Presuming God's Care and Compassion

1. In the psalms you will discover God's care for you. You will discover that He hears your prayers. How did you see the Lord's care and His response in Psalm 66?

2. What was your favorite quote from today's study?

DAY 5: Personalizing God's Presence

1. On day 5 you learned the importance of personalizing what you learn about God. What does that mean, and why do you think getting personal with God is so important in the experience of power in prayer?

2. What did you learn about God from your reading in the Word today?

3. What was your favorite quote from today's study?

DAYS 6 AND 7: Devotional Reading by Eugene Peterson

1. What was your favorite verse, insight, or quote from your quiet times this week?

2. What did you learn from the excerpt by Eugene Peterson?

3. What is the most important truth you learned this week about prayer? How can you apply it in your own life?

Week Two: Prayer When You Want to Adore God

DAY 1: Blessing the Lord

Begin today by summarizing what everyone learned in week 1 about the priority of prayer and prayer in the psalms. This week we looked at what it means to adore God.

1. Ask your group what they learned from the life of Isaac Watts—who was he, and what was his contribution for our life of prayer?

2. Psalm 104 was our main area of study for this week. What was your favorite verse in Psalm 104?

3. What does it mean to bless the Lord?

4. What kinds of things can we say to the Lord that blesses Him?

DAY 2: For Who He Is

1. How does knowing who God is help you adore Him more?

2. What did you learn about God today from your study in His Word?

3. What are the most important truths you've learned about God in your adventure with Him?

4. What was your favorite quote from the devotional readings by Tozer and Smith?

DAY 3: For What He Does

1. What was your most significant insight about God in Psalm 104?

2. What was your favorite quote in your quiet time today?

3. Where do you need to trust God, and how does knowing what God can do help you?

DAY 4: For His Eternal Glory

1. What was the most important truth you learned about God's glory?

2. How does knowing about God's glory help you in adoring Him?

DAY 5: Eternal Praise and Gladness

1. How does praise and gladness change the weight of trials and difficulties?

2. What did you learn from the experience of Darlene Zschech and her husband?

3. You had the opportunity to look at the song of the Lord throughout the psalms. What did you learn about your song to the Lord?

DAYS 6 AND 7: Devotional Reading by Andrew Murray

1. What was your favorite verse, insight, or quote from your quiet times this week?

2. What did you learn from the excerpt by Andrew Murray?

3. What is the most important truth you learned about adoring God this week? How can you apply it in your own life, and how will it help you adore God more?

Week Three: Prayer When You Need to Confess Sin

DAY 1: The Ground of Your Forgiveness

1. Open your discussion with prayer. Share briefly about your discussion last week about adoring God.

2. Why does knowing God become such a humbling experience for us?

3. Why is David such an example for us in knowing how to confess sin? What was his sin, and how did he confess it?

4. Why are you able to be forgiven? What is the ground of your forgiveness?

5. What did you learn about grace?

6. You learned that God's throne is a throne of grace. How do you need to draw near to the throne of grace—where do you need God's help today?

DAY 2: The Nature of Confession

1. What did you learn from the story about Mackay in Prepare Your Heart?

2. What does it mean to confess sin?

3. What was your favorite quote today?

DAY 3: The Joy of Restoration and Renewal

1. In day 3 you learned about the joy of forgiveness. What did you learn about the joy of forgiveness from David in his psalms?

2. How does the cleansing of God by forgiving your sins restore and renew you?

DAY 4: The Power of the Spirit

1. How does the Holy Spirit make a difference in our lives?

2. What was your favorite quote from your quiet time today?

DAY 5: The Beauty of Humility

1. Describe what it means to have a humble heart. Why is humility so beautiful?

2. What was the most profound truth you learned from the parable about the tax collector?

3. What did you learn about humility in the verses in your quiet time today?

4. David has been your prayer partner this week. What have you learned from him that will help you in confessing sin?

DAYS 6 AND 7: Devotional Reading by Brennan Manning

1. In days 6 and 7 you had the opportunity to read a prayer by Brennan Manning. What was your favorite truth from his prayer?

2. What was your favorite insight, quote, or verse from your quiet times this week?

3. What was the most important truth that you learned about confession of sin?

Week Four: Prayer When You Want to Say Thank You

DAY 1: The Resolve of Thanksgiving

1. Open your discussion with prayer. Share briefly about your discussion last week regarding confession of sin.

2. This week we had the opportunity to look at David's example of how to thank God. What was the most important insight you learned from David this week?

3. What was most significant to you about the healing of the lepers? What can you learn from that event to help you in your own relationship with the Lord?

4. What is the value of making a resolve or a commitment to thank the Lord? Why is such a resolve or commitment important?

5. What was your favorite quote from your quiet time today?

DAY 2: The Reverence of Thanksgiving

1. In day 2 you saw the relationship of reverence to thanksgiving. What does it mean to be reverent, and how will it help you in thanking God?

2. What was your favorite phrase from Amy Carmichael's prayer?

3. What was your favorite translation of Psalm 138:2? How does reading different translations help you understand the meaning of a verse?

4. What was most significant to you in the devotion of the woman with the alabaster jar in Luke 7:36-50?

5. How does God's Word help you to have a heart of devotion?

DAY 3: The Response to Thanksgiving

1. What was the result when David expressed thanksgiving to the Lord?

2. What did you learn from your study in God's Word about finding strength in the Lord?

3. How have you experienced strength from the Lord?

4. What was your favorite quote in your quiet time today?

DAY 4: The Revival in Thanksgiving

1. How does a thankful heart help you experience personal spiritual revival from the Lord?

2. What did you learn about revival from your time in God's Word in day 4?

3. What was your favorite quote in day 4?

4. You read Henry Law's words about how the Lord will strengthen and refresh us and

cause our graces to blossom like a rose. How has the Lord refreshed you and caused you to blossom like a rose?

DAY 5: The Reliance Through Thanksgiving

1. What did you learn about gratitude and thanksgiving from the story about the balloonist in Prepare Your Heart?

2. How do David's words "The LORD will accomplish what concerns me" (Psalm 138:8) encourage you?

3. The Lord desires your trust in Him. Why do we worry instead of trust sometimes?

4. What did you learn from your time in God's Word that will help you trust the Lord?

DAYS 6 AND 7: Devotional Reading by Isaac Watts

1. In days 6 and 7 you had the opportunity to read from Isaac Watts. What was your favorite truth from his writing?

2. What was the most important truth you learned from this week?

3. Did you have a favorite quote? A favorite verse?

4. Close in prayer.

Week Five: Prayer When You Want to Ask God

DAY 1: For God's Answer

1. Open your discussion with prayer. Share briefly about your discussion last week on David and prayer of thanks to the Lord.

2. This week, we looked at asking God for things in prayer. David was your prayer partner in helping you learn how to pray and what to pray. Read the quote by James McConkey at the beginning of week 5.

3. In day 1, you looked at the importance of expecting God's answer. What was

impressive to you about God's answer to prayer in the circumstance involving Tony Campolo?

4. Describe what you learned about David's life situation, which prompted him to pray the words of Psalm 143.

5. Describe the plan for prayer according to the acrostic ACTS.

6. How does confession pave the way for asking God for our needs?

7. What was your favorite verse in your quiet time in Day 1?

8. What was your favorite quote from Ole Hallesby?

DAY 2: For Teaching

1. One of the first requests you learned from David was asking God to teach you. What does it mean to be teachable?

2. How did you see a teachable heart in David, and what did he want to learn?

3. What did David want to learn according to Psalm 25?

4. What do you want to learn from the Lord?

DAY 3: For Guidance

1. In day 3 you learned about God's leading in your life. What impressed you about the story from Billy Graham's life?

2. What did you learn about God's leading and guidance from your study in God's Word?

3. How do you need the Lord's guidance today?

DAY 4: For Personal Revival

1. David taught you a very important prayer in Psalm 143:11: *Revive me.* What are you asking for when you pray for revival?

2. What did you learn about revival from the verses you read in the psalms?

3. How have you experienced personal revival in the past? How do you need revival today?

DAY 5: For Deliverance

1. In day 5 you learned that sometimes you need to be patient in prayer until you are delivered. In Prepare Your Heart you learned about "praying through" in your prayers. What does that mean?

2. God is a God of deliverances. What did you learn about deliverance from your study in the Bible?

3. What was your favorite quote in your quiet time?

4. Where in your life do you need deliverance?

DAYS 6 AND 7: Devotional Reading by Charles Spurgeon

1. What was your favorite verse, insight, or quote from your quiet times this week?

2. What did you learn from the excerpt written by Charles Spurgeon?

3. What is the most important truth you learned about prayer this week? How can you apply it in your own life, and how will it help you ask God for the needs in your life and the lives of others?

4. Close by reading together the prayer by Amy Carmichael on day 5 in Adore God in Prayer.

Week Six: Prayer When You Are in Trouble

DAY 1: Where Do You Run?

1. Open your discussion with prayer. Share briefly about your discussion last week regarding asking God for things in prayer. Summarize what you learned about all the different requests you can take to the Lord.

2. This week we have focused on what to pray when we are in trouble. Begin by reading the quote from *Streams in the Desert* at the beginning of week 6.

3. What meant the most to you from the story about Jim Cymbala's daughter Chrissy? What did you learn about prayer from his experience?

4. In day 1 you began a week in Psalm 77, written by Asaph. Who was Asaph, and what did you learn about his suffering in Psalm 77?

5. How does Asaph, as your prayer partner, help you learn what to do when you are in trouble?

6. What did you learn in your quiet time about God's help in times of trouble?

DAY 2: Will You Remember?

1. In day 2 you learned the importance of remembering when you are in a time of trouble. What does it mean to remember?

2. What did Asaph remember?

3. Why is setting aside time with the Lord important to help you remember?

4. Asaph remembered his song in the night. As you looked at the different verses about the song from the Lord, what was your favorite verse or phrase?

5. You had the opportunity to write your own song to the Lord. Would you like to share your song?

DAY 3: What Has God Promised?

1. How do the promises of God help you in a time of trouble?

2. How did Asaph struggle with what he knew to be true about God and His Word? Where do you experience the greatest struggle in standing on the promises of God?

3. What did you learn about the value of God's Word and its importance in your own life?

4. You had the opportunity to read Jeremiah 17:5-89. What happens when you trust in the Lord?

5. What was your favorite quote from today's quiet time?

DAY 4: Who Is Your God?

1. In Asaph's time of trouble, he turned his thoughts to contemplating God. What did you learn about God in Psalm 77, and how does this encourage you?

2. What was your favorite quote in your quiet time in day 4?

DAY 5: What Has God Done?

1. How does knowing what God can do encourage you in a time of trouble?

2. What did you learn from your time in God's Word about what God can do?

3. What did you learn from Spurgeon and *Streams in the Desert* that will help you pray in a time of trouble?

DAYS 6 AND 7: Devotional Reading by John Henry Jowett

1. What was your favorite verse, insight, or quote from your quiet times this week?

2. What did you learn from the excerpt by John Henry Jowett?

3. What is the most important truth you learned about prayer this week? How can you apply it in your own life, and how will what you have learned help you pray when you are in trouble?

4. Close in prayer.

Week Seven: Prayer When You Are Thirsty

DAY 1: When You Are in the Wilderness

1. Open your discussion with prayer. Share briefly about all that we have been learning from the psalmists about prayer. What makes the writers of the psalms such good prayer partners?

2. In week 7, we looked at the kind of prayer we need when we are thirsty and in a wilderness experience. Begin by reading Psalm 63:1. What did you learn about the wilderness? Describe the wilderness experiences of life.

3. Have you ever been in a wilderness experience, and if so, how did God meet you and work in your life?

4. What words from David in Psalm 63 give us the idea he was in a wilderness experience?

5. What did you learn from your study in God's Word about the wilderness?

6. What was your favorite quote in your quiet time?

DAY 2: Praise Him in the Wilderness

1. David was able to praise God in his wilderness. What was the subject of his praise?

2. What did you learn about God's love and how does His love inspire you to praise Him?

DAY 3: Remember Him in the Wilderness

1. David remembered the Lord in the night. How does his example encourage you?

2. What was your favorite insight from Psalm 42 that will help you pray when you are in a wilderness?

DAY 4: Cling to Him in the Wilderness

1. In day 4 you saw the importance of clinging to the Lord in the wilderness. What was your favorite phrase by Gerhard Tersteegen in Prepare Your Heart?

2. What does it mean to cling to the Lord, and why is clinging to Him so important in the wilderness?

3. What did you learn from your time in God's Word that will help you to cling to the Lord?

4. What was significant about Jeremiah's waistband, and what did it teach you about clinging to the Lord? How important is your clinging to the Lord to God Himself?

DAY 5: Glorify Him in the Wilderness

1. When you are in a wilderness, you can bring glory to the Lord. What does bringing glory to God mean?

2. What did you learn about glory in God's Word today?

3. What did you learn from Henry Law in your quiet time?

DAYS 6 AND 7: Devotional Reading by James H. McConkey

1. What was your favorite verse, insight, or quote from your quiet times this week?

2. What did you learn from the excerpt written by James McConkey?

3. What is the most important truth you learned about prayer this week? How can you apply it in your own life, and how will it help you pray when you are in a wilderness experience?

Week Eight: *Prayer When You Want to Go Higher*

DAY 1: Prayer from the Depths to the Heights

1. Open with prayer. Then begin your discussion by expressing how much you've enjoyed leading the group and sharing together during this quiet time experience. Share how wonderful the discussions have been. Encourage your class or group to not miss out on the companion 30-day journey of *Passionate Prayer.* As you talk together for one last time, ask your group what has been their favorite part of this study.

2. This week you had the opportunity to look at the prayer when you want to go higher. What desire are you expressing in the prayer to go higher?

3. What are the Psalms of Ascent, and how will they help make us passionate in our prayers to the Lord?

4. How do you need to pray when you are in the depths of life? How did the examples of prayer in the psalms you read in day 1 help you?

5. What was your favorite quote in your devotional reading in day 1?

DAY 2: The Prayer of Supplication

1. The psalmist prayed, "Let Your ears be attentive to the voice of my supplication." What does supplication mean?

2. What did you learn about the prayer of supplication from your study in God's Word in day 2?

3. How did the words of E.M. Bounds encourage you to pray?

4. What is one of your biggest requests of the Lord right now?

DAY 3: The Prayer Because of Grace

1. What is grace, and why do you need it when you want to pray to go higher?

2. What did you learn about the grace of God? What was your favorite verse about God's grace?

DAY 4: The Prayer of Waiting

1. In day 4 you studied the prayer of waiting. Why is waiting so difficult sometimes?

2. What does it mean to wait on the Lord?

3. What did you learn from the verses in the psalms about waiting on the Lord?

4. What did you learn from the example of Moses in Psalm 90?

5. What was your favorite quote from the devotional reading in day 4?

DAY 5: The Prayer of Hope

1. What is hope, and how will hope help you pray and take you deeper in your relationship with the Lord?

2. How do the promises of God help you hope? What promises did the writer of Psalm 130 trust?

3. What did you learn about hope from your study in God's Word?

4. What was your favorite quote in the devotional reading in day 5?

5. How did God answer the prayer that you wrote in your letter to Him at the beginning of this study?

6. What will you take with you from this quiet time experience? What will you always remember?

DAYS 6 AND 7: Devotional Reading by Octavius Winslow

1. What was your favorite verse, insight, or quote from your quiet times this week and from the entire book of quiet times?

2. What encouraged you from the excerpt by Octavius Winslow?

3. How has your time in Psalms helped you learn more about prayer? Why are the psalmists such wonderful prayer partners?

4. Close in prayer.

≈ NOTES ≈

WEEK ONE

Epigraph. Dietrich Bonhoeffer, *Life Together* (San Francisco: Harper & Row, 1954), 47.

1. James H. McConkey, *Prayer* (Pittsburgh: Silver Publishing Society, 1931), 7-8.

2. S.D. Gordon, *Quiet Talks on Prayer* (New York: Revell, 1904), 12-13.

3. Oswald Chambers, *My Utmost for His Highest* (many editions). See the entry for August 23.

4. Henry Law, *Daily Prayer and Praise* (Carlisle, PA: Banner of Truth Trust, 2000), 152.

5. Arthur Bennett, ed., *The Valley of Vision: A Collection of Puritan Prayers and Devotion* (Carlisle, PA: Banner of Truth Trust, 1994), 11.

6. Ole Hallesby, *Prayer* (Minneapolis: Augsburg, 1931), 140-41.

7. Andrew Murray, *The Best of Andrew Murray* (Uhrichsville, OH: Barbour, 2000). See the entry for December 16.

8. George Watson, *Soul Food* (Cincinnati: Knapp, 1896). Quoted in Mrs. Charles E. Cowman, *Streams in the Desert* (Los Angeles: The Oriental Missionary Society, 1925). See the entry for April 5.

9. Charles T. Cook, ed., *Behold the Throne of Grace: C.H. Spurgeon's Prayers and Hymns* (London: Marshall, Morgan & Scott), 20.

10. Eugene Peterson, *Answering God* (San Francisco: HarperSanFrancisco, 1989), 5.

11. Hallesby, *Prayer,* 144.

12. Hallesby, *Prayer,* 145.

13. Hallesby, *Prayer,* 145.

14. Peterson, *Answering God,* 56, 128.

WEEK TWO

Epigraph. *The NIV Worship Bible* (Dana Point, CA: The Corinthian Group, 2000), 691.

1. J.M.K., *Bright Talks on Favourite Hymns* (London: The Religious Tract Society, 1916), 98.

2. Quoted in J.M.K., *Bright Talks on Favourite Hymns,* 98.

3. A.W. Tozer, *Man, the Dwelling Place of God* (Camp Hill, PA: Christian Publications, 1992), 76.

4. Herbert Lockyer, *Psalms: A Devotional Commentary* (Grand Rapids: Kregel, 1993), 402.

5. Isaac Watts, *A Guide to Prayer* (Carlisle, PA: Banner of Truth Trust, 2001), 12.

6. A.W. Tozer, *The Knowledge of the Holy* (New York: Harper & Row, 1961), 50.

7. Hannah Whitall Smith, *The God of All Comfort* (Chicago: Moody Press, 1956), 14-15.

8. Law, *Daily Prayer and Praise,* 108.

9. Tozer, *The Knowledge of the Holy,* 73.

10. Watts, *A Guide to Prayer,* 13.

11. F.B. Meyer, *Daily Prayers* (Wheaton: Shaw, 1995), 18.

12. John Calvin, *Heart Aflame: Daily Readings from Calvin on the Psalms* (Phillipsburg: P&R, 1999), 57.

13. Darlene Zschech, *Extravagant Worship: Holy, Holy, Holy Is the Lord God Almighty Who Was and Is, and Is to Come* (Minneapolis: Bethany House, 2001), 58-59.

14. Calvin, *Heart Aflame,* 265.

15. Andrew Murray, *God's Best Secrets* (New Kensington, PA: Whitaker House 1998), 82.

WEEK THREE

Epigraph. Murray, *God's Best Secrets,* 22.

1. Charles Spurgeon, New Park Street Chapel sermon delivered on January 7, 1855; quoted in J.I. Packer, *Knowing God* (Downers Grove, IL: InterVarsity Press, 1973), 13.

2. William Newell, *Romans Verse by Verse* (Chicago: Moody Press, 1977), 115.

3. Miles J. Stanford, *Principles of Spiritual Growth* (Lincoln: Back to the Bible, 1987), 18.

4. Murray, *God's Best Secrets,* 22.

5. Ian Malins, *Prepare the Way for Revival: Essential Keys That Bring God's Manifest Presence* (Grand Rapids: Chosen Books, 2004), 82-83.

6. Larry Richards, *The 365 Day Devotional Commentary* (Wheaton: Victor Books, 1990), 342.

7. Quoted in Robert Parsons, ed., *Quotes from the Quiet Hour* (Chicago: Moody Press 1949), 37.

8. Law, *Daily Prayer and Praise,* 255.

9. Selwyn Hughes, *Every Day Light: Water for the Soul* (Nashville: B&H, 1998), 3.

10. Murray, *God's Best Secrets,* 24.

11. A.W. Tozer, *The Divine Conquest* (New York: Revell, 1950), 128.

12. Cowman, *Streams in the Desert,* 270.

13. Andrew Murray, *Humility: The Beauty of Holiness* (Old Tappan: Revell, 1961), 36.

14. Brennan Manning, *The Ragamuffin Gospel: Embracing the Unconditional Love of God* (Sisters, OR: Multnomah, 2000), 139.

WEEK FOUR

Epigraph. Hallesby, *Prayer,* 137.

1. Catherine Marshall, ed., *The Prayers of Peter Marshall* (New York: McGraw-Hill, 1949), 29.

2. Hallesby, *Prayer,* 138-39.

3. Amy Carmichael, *Mountain Breezes* (Fort Washington: Christian Literature Crusade, 1999), 33-34.

4. Zschech, *Extravagant Worship,* 26-27.

5. Hallesby, *Prayer,* 138-40.

6. William B. Sprague, *Lectures on Revivals of Religion* (Birmingham: Solid Ground Christian Books, 2005), 7-8.

7. Norman Grubb, *Continuous Revival* (Fort Washington: Christian Literature Crusade, 1997), 8-9.

8. Bruce Larson and Lloyd J. Ogilvie, *Luke,* vol. 26, *The Preacher's Commentary Series* (Nashville: Nelson, 1983), 252.

9. Watts, *A Guide to Prayer,* 31-32.

WEEK FIVE

Epigraph. McConkey, *Prayer,* 87.

1. Derek Kidner, *Psalms* (Downers Grove: InterVarsity Press, 1973), 475.

2. Hallesby, *Prayer,* 144-45.

3. Charles Spurgeon, *The Treasury of David,* vol. 3 (McLean, VA: MacDonald, n.d.), 348.

4. Wesley L. Duewel, *Mighty Prevailing Prayer* (Grand Rapids, MI: Zondervan, 1990), 10-11.

5. Charles Spurgeon, *Morning and Evening* (Peabody, MA: Hendrickson, 2006). See the evening entry for June 17.

6. Adapted from Mrs. Charles Cowman, *Springs in the Valley* (Los Angeles: The Oriental Missionary Society, 1939), 66-67.

7. Amy Carmichael, *Toward Jerusalem* (Fort Washington: Christian Literature Crusade, 1936), 52.

8. McConkey, *Prayer,* 100-101.

9. Quoted in Cowman, *Springs in the Valley,* 66-67.

10. Charles Spurgeon, *The Power of Prayer in a Believer's Life* (Lynnwood, WA: Emerald Books, 1993), 104.

WEEK SIX

Epigraph. Quoted in Cowman, *Streams in the Desert,* 162.

1. Adapted from Jim Cymbala, *Fresh Wind, Fresh Fire* (Grand Rapids: Zondervan , 1997), 63-66.

2. Law, *Daily Prayer and Praise,* 4.

3. Spurgeon, *The Treasury of David,* vol. 2, 320-21.

4. Alan Redpath, *The Making of a Man of God* (Old Tappan, NJ: Revell, 1962), 5.

5. Quoted in Cowman, *Streams in the Desert,* 107-8.

6. Meyer, *Daily Prayers,* 83.

7. Smith, *The God of All Comfort,* 109, 120-21.

8. Law, *Daily Prayer and Praise,* 7.

9. Marshall, *The Prayers of Peter Marshall,* 18.

10. Cook, ed., *Behold the Throne of Grace,* 15.

11. Quoted in Cowman, *Streams in the Desert,* 77-78.

12. Quoted in Cowman, *Springs in the Valley,* 204-5.

13. Law, *Daily Prayer and Praise,* 9.

14. Quoted in *Springs in the Valley,* 204-5.

15. John Henry Jowett, *Springs in the Desert* (Grand Rapids: Baker Book House, 1924), 151-53.

WEEK SEVEN

Epigraph. Quoted in Cowman, *Streams in the Desert,* 2.

1. A.W. Tozer, *The Pursuit of God* (Camp Hill, PA: Christian Publications, 1982), 20.

2. F.B. Meyer, *Devotional Commentary* (Wheaton: Tyndale House, 1989), 304.

3. Quoted in Cowman, *Streams in the Desert,* 38-39.

4. Tommy Barnett, et. al., *The Desert Experience* (Nashville: Nelson, 2001), 114-15.

5. Spurgeon, *Morning and Evening.* See the evening entry for July 21.

6. Spurgeon, *Morning and Evening.* See the evening entry for July 21.

7. Meyer, *Devotional Commentary,* 247.

8. Quoted in A.W. Tozer, *The Christian Book of Mystical Verse* (Camp Hill, PA: Christian Publications, 1963), 57-58.

9. Meyer, *Daily Prayers,* 102.

10. Law, *Daily Prayer and Praise,* 301.

11. Law, *Daily Prayer and Praise,* 300-301.

12. Quoted in Tozer, *The Christian Book of Mystical Verse,* 59.

13. McConkey, *Prayer,* 100.

WEEK EIGHT

Epigraph. Author unknown, *The Kneeling Christian* (Grand Rapids: Zondervan, 1971), 56.

1. Watchman Nee, *Christian Reader,* vol. 34, n.p.

2. James Montgomery Boice, *Psalms,* vol. 3 (Grand Rapids: Baker Book House, 1998), 1070.

3. Quoted in Cook, ed., *Behold the Throne of Grace,* 59-60.

4. Octavius Winslow, *Help Heavenward* (Carlisle, PA: Banner of Truth Trust, 2000), 70-72.

5. E.M. Bounds, *Power Through Prayer* (Minneapolis: World Wide Publications, 1989), 36.

6. Octavius Winslow, *Christ's Sympathy to Weary Pilgrims* (Pensacola, FL: Chapel Library), 29.

7. J. Vernon McGee, *Thru the Bible Commentary: Poetry (Psalms 90–150)* (Nashille: Nelson, 1991), 127.

8. Matthew Henry and Thomas Scott, *Matthew Henry's Concise Commentary* CD ROM (Oak Harbor, WA: Logos Research Systems, 1997). See the commentary on Romans 5:1.

9. Author unknown. Quoted in D.L. Moody, *The Joy of Answered Prayer* (New Kensington, PA: Whitaker House, 1997), 118.

10. Quoted in Cowman, *Streams in the Desert,* 341.

11. Meyer, *Daily Prayers,* 30.

12. Andrew Murray, *Waiting on God* (New Kensington, PA: Whitaker House, 1981), 112-13.

13. Matthew Henry, *Experiencing God's Presence* (New Kensington, PA: Whitaker House 1997), 61.

14. F.B. Meyer, *Choice Notes on the Psalms* (Grand Rapids: Kregel, 1984), 157.

15. John Oxenham, "God's Handwriting," in *Bees in Amber: A Little Book of Thoughtful Verse.* Available online at www.gutenberg.org/ebooks/9989.

16. Spurgeon, *Morning and Evening.* See the entry for the morning of January 6.

17. Quoted in Cowman, *Streams in the Desert,* 337-38.

18. Winslow, *Help Heavenward,* 171-85.

❧ ACKNOWLEDGMENTS ❧

I want to thank the Lord first and foremost for entrusting the writing of these quiet times to me. What a privilege. Thank you to my precious family—my great encouragement during the writing—David, Mother, Dad, Rob, Tania, Kayla, Christopher, Eloise, Andy, Keegan, and James. A special thanks to my dear husband, who is the most brilliant person I know. David, your insights and wisdom are without equal. Thank you for loving me.

I am especially thankful to the entire team at Harvest House Publishers. Working with you on these books is one of God's greatest blessings in my life. Thank you, Bob Hawkins Jr., president of Harvest House, for your vision and steadfast commitment to the Lord. You are a great example for me of a Hebrews 13:7 kind of person. Thank you, Terry Glaspey, for encouraging me to write the books on my heart and mind. And Gene Skinner, thank you for your impeccable editing and your heart for the Lord.

I am so very thankful to our Quiet Time Ministries staff team for serving the Lord together with me—Kayla Branscum, Paula Zillmer, Shirley Peters, Conni Hudson, Cindy Clark, and Kelly Abeyratne. A special thanks to Kayla and Charlie Branscum, who serve tirelessly and faithfully with me at our Resource and Training Center.

Thank you to all who joined me in piloting this book of quiet times.

And then, thank you to my dear friends who have so faithfully prayed for me and with me: Beverly Trupp, Andy Graybill, Dottie McDowell, Vonette Bright, Julie Airis, Helen Peck, Stefanie Kelly, Carolyn Haynes, John and Betty Mann, Sandi Rogers, Myra Murphy, and Kathleen Otremba.

Thank you to the board of directors of Quiet Time Ministries, the *Enriching Your Quiet Time* magazine staff, and those who partner financially and prayerfully together with me in Quiet Time Ministries.

A special thank you to Shannon Wexelberg for your *Faithful God* CD, an important encouragement to me as I wrote both the *Passionate Prayer* 30-Day Journey and A Quiet Time Experience.

Thank you to the staff at Southwest Community Church for loving the Lord. A special thanks to Shelley Smith, our women's ministries assistant, for your tireless service and commitment to our Lord. And thank you to the women at Southwest Community Church—it is such a joy and privilege to serve the Lord together with you.

And then, thank you to those who have been such a huge help to me all along the way in the writing and publishing of books: Jim Smoke—your friendship has been so important to me, and oh, how I thank the Lord for you. Greg Johnson, my agent at WordServe Literary—your encouragement and wisdom has been invaluable to me in the running of my race.

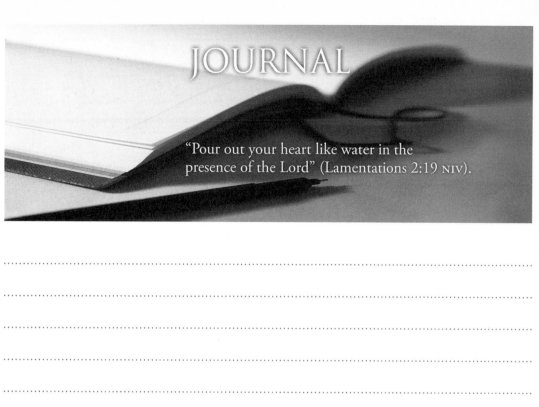

JOURNAL

"Pour out your heart like water in the presence of the Lord" (Lamentations 2:19 NIV).

JOURNAL

"Pour out your heart like water in the presence of the Lord" (Lamentations 2:19 NIV).

JOURNAL

"Pour out your heart like water in the presence of the Lord" (Lamentations 2:19 NIV).

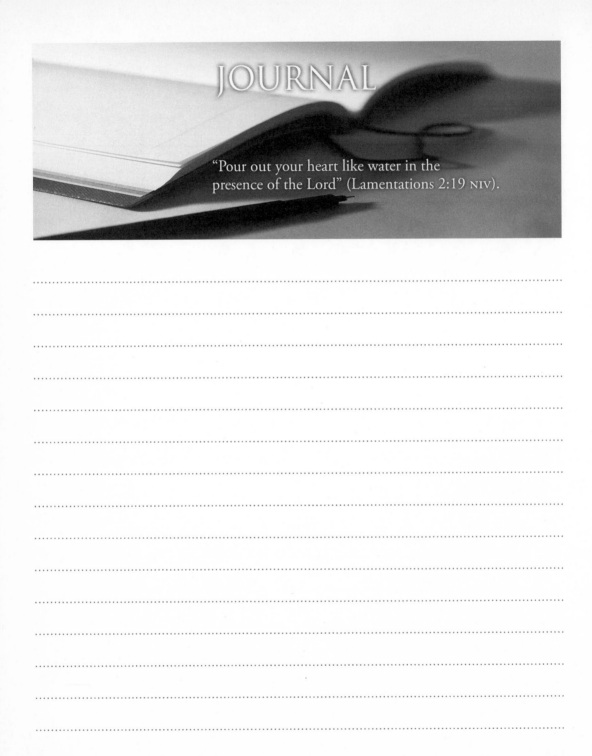

JOURNAL

"Pour out your heart like water in the presence of the Lord" (Lamentations 2:19 NIV).

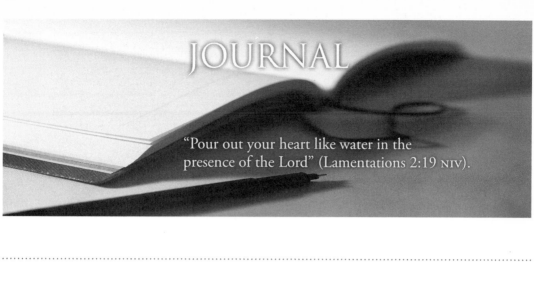

JOURNAL

"Pour out your heart like water in the presence of the Lord" (Lamentations 2:19 NIV).

JOURNAL

"Pour out your heart like water in the presence of the Lord" (Lamentations 2:19 NIV).

ADORE GOD IN PRAYER

"Don't worry about anything;
instead, pray about everything" (Philippians 4:6 NLT).

*Prayer for*_____

Date: Topic:

Scripture:

Request:

Answer:

Date: Topic:

Scripture:

Request:

Answer:

Date: Topic:

Scripture:

Request:

Answer:

Date: Topic:

Scripture:

Request:

Answer:

Date: Topic:

Scripture:

Request:

Answer:

ADORE GOD IN PRAYER

"Don't worry about anything;
instead, pray about everything" (Philippians 4:6 NLT).

*Prayer for*_____

Date: Topic:
Scripture:
Request:

Answer:

_____

Date: Topic:
Scripture:
Request:

Answer:

_____

Date: Topic:
Scripture:
Request:

Answer:

_____

Date: Topic:
Scripture:
Request:

Answer:

_____

Date: Topic:
Scripture:
Request:

Answer:

_____

ADORE GOD IN PRAYER

"Don't worry about anything;
instead, pray about everything" (Philippians 4:6 NLT).

*Prayer for*_____

Date: Topic:
Scripture:
Request:

Answer:

Date: Topic:
Scripture:
Request:

Answer:

Date: Topic:
Scripture:
Request:

Answer:

Date: Topic:
Scripture:
Request:

Answer:

Date: Topic:
Scripture:
Request:

Answer:

ADORE GOD IN PRAYER

"Don't worry about anything;
instead, pray about everything" (Philippians 4:6 NLT).

Prayer for_____

Date: Topic:
Scripture:
Request:

Answer:

Date: Topic:
Scripture:
Request:

Answer:

Date: Topic:
Scripture:
Request:

Answer:

Date: Topic:
Scripture:
Request:

Answer:

Date: Topic:
Scripture:
Request:

Answer:

ADORE GOD IN PRAYER

"Don't worry about anything;
instead, pray about everything" (Philippians 4:6 NLT).

*Prayer for*_____

Date: Topic:

Scripture:

Request:

Answer:

_____

Date: Topic:

Scripture:

Request:

Answer:

_____

Date: Topic:

Scripture:

Request:

Answer:

_____

Date: Topic:

Scripture:

Request:

Answer:

_____

Date: Topic:

Scripture:

Request:

Answer:

_____

ADORE GOD IN PRAYER

"Don't worry about anything;
instead, pray about everything" (Philippians 4:6 NLT).

*Prayer for*_____

Date: Topic:
Scripture:
Request:

Answer:

_____

Date: Topic:
Scripture:
Request:

Answer:

_____

Date: Topic:
Scripture:
Request:

Answer:

_____

Date: Topic:
Scripture:
Request:

Answer:

_____

Date: Topic:
Scripture:
Request:

Answer:

_____